The Bassoon, How It Works

The Bassoon, How It Works

A Practical Guide to Bassoon Ownership

Michael J. Pagliaro

Co-Published in Partnership with the
National Association for Music Education

ROWMAN & LITTLEFIELD
Lanham • Boulder • New York • London

Published by Rowman & Littlefield
An imprint of The Rowman & Littlefield Publishing Group, Inc.
4501 Forbes Boulevard, Suite 200, Lanham, Maryland 20706
www.rowman.com

86-90 Paul Street, London EC2A 4NE

Copyright © 2024 by The Rowman & Littlefield Publishing Group, Inc.

All rights reserved. No part of this book may be reproduced in any form or by any electronic or mechanical means, including information storage and retrieval systems, without written permission from the publisher, except by a reviewer who may quote passages in a review.

British Library Cataloguing in Publication Information Available

Library of Congress Cataloging-in-Publication Data

ISBN: 978-1-5381-9084-5 (pbk)
ISBN: 978-1-5381-9085-2 (ebook)

Table of Contents

Acknowledgments iv

Introduction v

1. What Are the Parts of My Bassoon? 1

2. How Does My Bassoon Work? 3

3. What Are the Different Kinds of Bassoons? 15

4. How Are Bassoons Made? 21

5. How Do I Take Care of My Bassoon? 29

6. How Should I Plan My Practice Sessions? 41

7. A Survey of the History of Woodwind Instruments 45

8. What Items (Accessories) Will I Need to Help Me Play My Bassoon? 65

Appendix 79

The Science of Sound 79
Glossary of Woodwind Instruments 85
Dictionary of Bassoon Terms 91
Index of Bassoon Parts 95
Instrument Ownership Record 97

Index 103

Acknowledgments

The following extraordinarily gifted musical instrument fabrication and distribution professionals have generously granted permission to use information and artwork from their websites. Listed in alphabetical order, they are:

Donna Altieri Bags, info@altieribags.com

Erick D. Brand, for permission to show the bassoon key system diagram from the Erick D. Brand Band Instrument Repair Manual

DoubleReed Ltd. UK, maker of high-quality bassoons, https:www.doublereed.co.uk

Fox Products Corporation, maker of hand-crafted double reed Instruments www.foxproducts.com

Vladislav Goncharov, maker of fine bassoons, atelier-goncharov.com

How It's Made, https://www.sciencechannel.com/show/how-its-made-bassoon

Lars Kirmser, publisher and musical instrument specialist at http://www.musictrader.com

Romain Picard, of the Buffet Crampon Keilwerth Company

John Stoner, President of the Conn-Selmer Company

Theo Wanne, for permission to use pictures from their website, mail@thore-woodwind.com

Rick Wilson, for permission to use his Historical Flute Page. http://www.oldflutes.com/boehm.htm

Schools WWBW, for permission to reproduce their bassoon fingering chart, schools@wwbw.com

Introduction

The method book you are now using was written to help you learn how to play the bassoon. That book contains information on holding your bassoon, making a sound, reading music, playing different notes, and much more.

This book will teach you additional information about your instrument to help you better understand how it works, how to work it, care for it, and how to be a more knowledgeable bassoonist.

The first section of this book reviews information that might be on the first few pages of your method book. Even if you know that information, spend a few moments reading this section to see if you can find something you have not yet learned. You will be learning information about the bassoon that not many students will ever know.

You do not have to read this book in the order in which the chapters appear. Start at any chapter that interests you, and then, as you progress, move to the chapters related to your bassoon studies. Because you can read any chapter, some needed information is repeated to cover the issue under study.

Chapter 1

What Are the Parts of My Bassoon?

The smallest section of the bassoon is the bocal (A). Made of metal, it connects the reed to the instrument's body. The body consists of the wing or tenor joint (B), boot or double joint (C), bass or long joint (D), and bell joint (E).

Because the bassoon is about eight feet long, it is folded in half at about the mid-point using a U-bend called the boot (C).

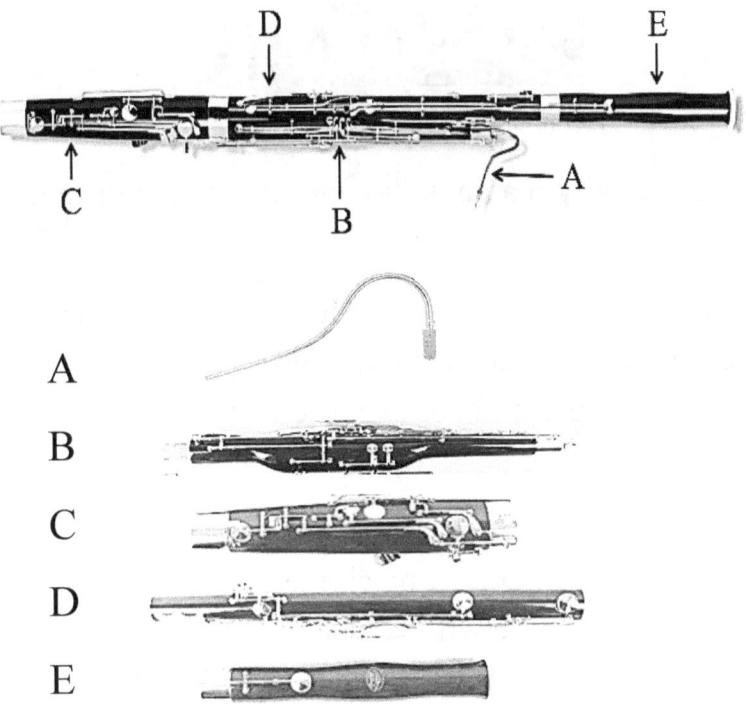

Corked tenons connect the five sections of the bassoon.

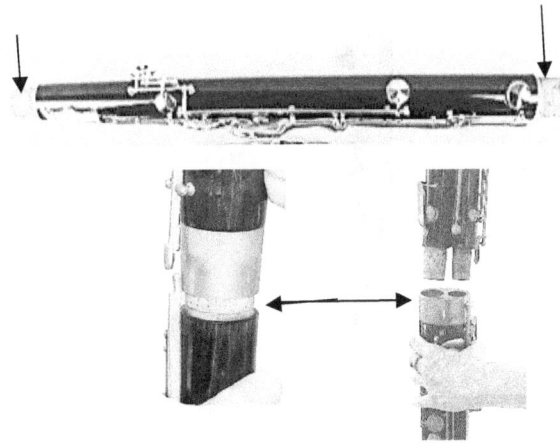

The body of the bassoon has a conical (cone-shaped) bore,

with tone holes operated by a mechanical padded key system.

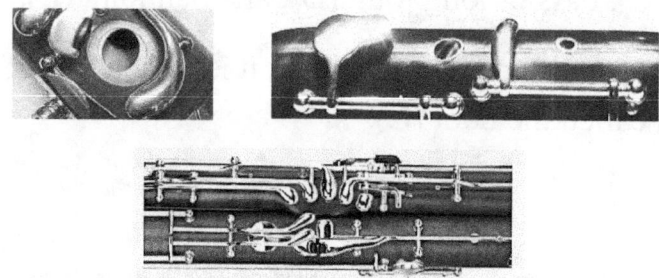

Bassoon bodies are usually maple, although other wood or man-made materials are also used.

Bassoons are now made in two types, the long-bore and short-bore models. The long-bore instrument produces a darker tone and is believed by many to produce truer intonation. The short-bore bassoon is more difficult to control and, therefore, less consistent in intonation.

An interesting design feature of the bassoon is that the tone holes at some points must travel as far as 2 inches (5 cm) to reach the bore. These must be drilled at an angle so the interior end of the hole will be positioned to get the correct pitches, and the outer end will allow you to span the distance with your fingers.

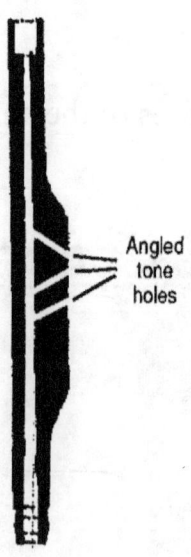

Angled tone holes

Chapter 2

How Does My Bassoon Work?

Sound Production

The sound generator for the bassoon is the double reed. There is no mouthpiece on a bassoon.

No two bassoon reeds produce exactly the same sound even though they are used by the same performer and on the same instrument. This is because good bassoon reeds are often individually made by hand and are the product of the skills or limitations of the maker.

In addition, the raw material, cane, is inconsistent and so delicate that a bassoon reed's life span is relatively short. This combination creates sound production problems on a bassoon that requires dedicated attention and expertise.

Bassoon reeds are made in different sizes, shapes, densities, and designs. There are usually ten parts to the design or shaping of the reed. Below is a diagram of the parts of a bassoon reed showing its two major sections, the lay and the tube. The tube is the base of the reed and is in contact with the bocal.

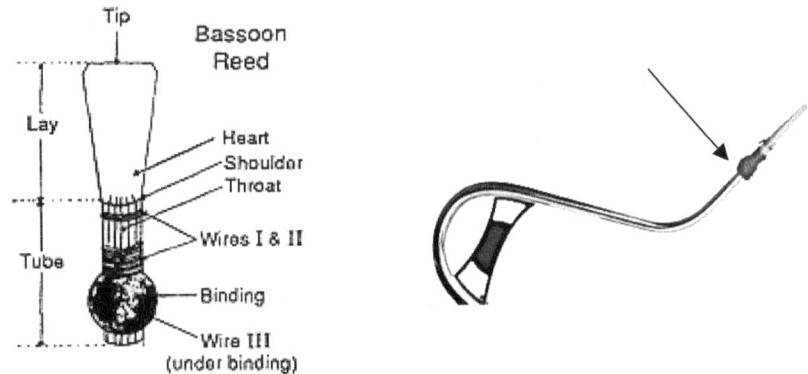

Bassoon Reed

The upper half, the lay, is the vibrating portion of the reed. The tip is the most sensitive part of the reed.

Bassoon reeds are grouped as being either German or French. The difference between them is in the thickness of the lay or heart of the reed. German reeds tend to be thicker in the heart, whereas French reeds have a more gradual and even taper.

This difference can be seen by holding the reed up to a strong light. You will notice that the center of the lay is shadowed on the German reed, whereas the light passes through more evenly on the French reed.

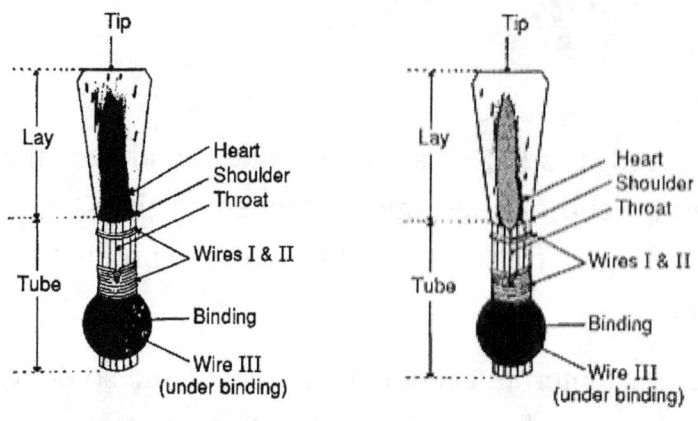

German Reed **French Reed**

You can also feel the difference by gently passing the heart of the reed between your thumb and index finger. The German reed will have a bulge down the center of the lay, while the French reed will feel flat. As a result of this structural difference, the French reed produces a thinner, more penetrating sound, while the German reed has a more haunting and darker sound.

Three shapes used in bassoon reed manufacturing are the parallel contour, the wedge type, and the double-wedge contour.

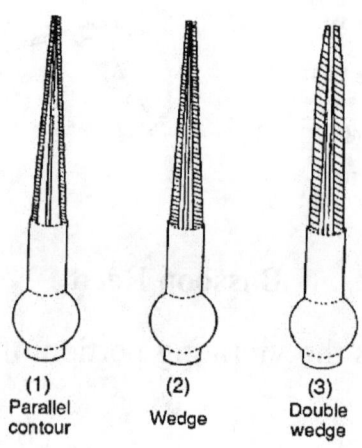

(1) Parallel contour   (2) Wedge   (3) Double wedge

The parallel shape (1) is constructed so that both blades have equal thickness throughout. This design is not commonly used because it is difficult to make and presents a problem to the player in maintaining pitch and tone quality control.

The wedge contour (2), where the blades gradually taper or thin out toward the tip, is used primarily in constructing the French-style reed. This design is more popular and easier to make.

The double-wedge contour (3), used for the German design reed, has many variations because it uses two degrees of taper. The first section of the blades shows a very slight taper or, sometimes, none. The second section of the blades then tapers more toward the tip of the reed. The length of the two taper sections can vary according to the needs of the player and the design used by the reed maker.

When you send a stream of air through a bassoon reed, the upper and lower blades vibrate, producing a sound. The reed staple (tube) carries a "raw" generated sound to the bore of the instrument and begins to become a tone. The sound from the reed sets the air column in the bassoon's body to vibrate, amplifying that sound.

Now, let's learn what happens to the sound you produce after it enters the bassoon.

The bassoon has a basic set of six tone holes on the front of the body. These are covered by keys fingered by each hand's index, middle, and third fingers. The pinky finger is used to finger the spatula keys. Pictured below are the front and back of a bassoon and the correct hand position.

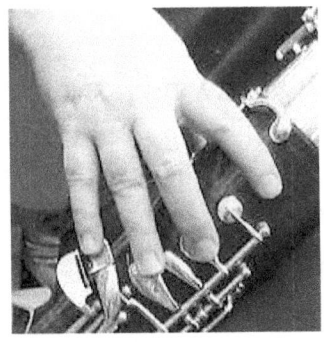 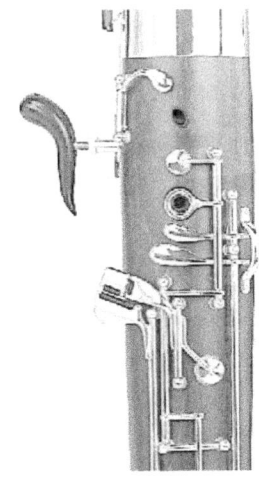 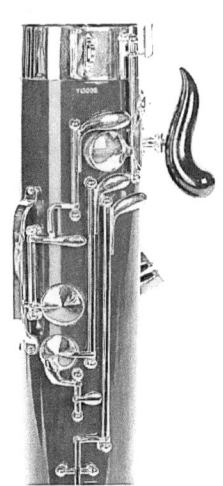

Additional tone holes are placed in other locations on the body to complete the notes on the instrument. These are covered by side keys, which are worked by the thumb, pinky finger, and the side of the index fingers between the first and second knuckle on each hand.

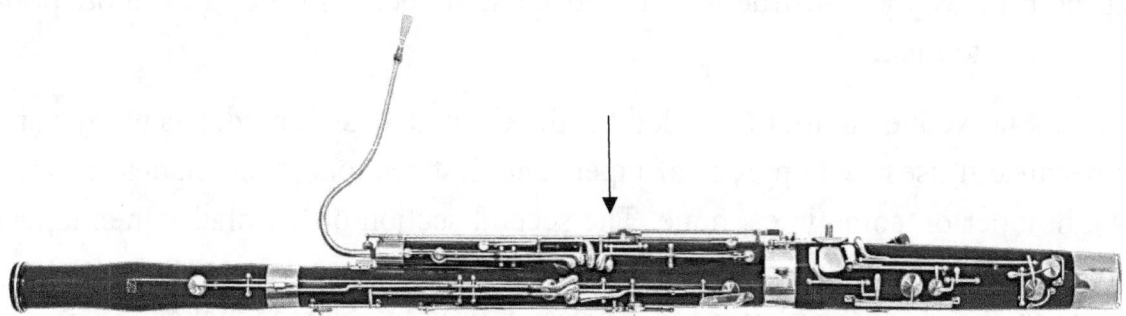

When you play the bassoon, the sound-producing length of the instrument is the distance between the reed and the first open hole. As you cover the holes, the instrument becomes longer, and the sound becomes lower.

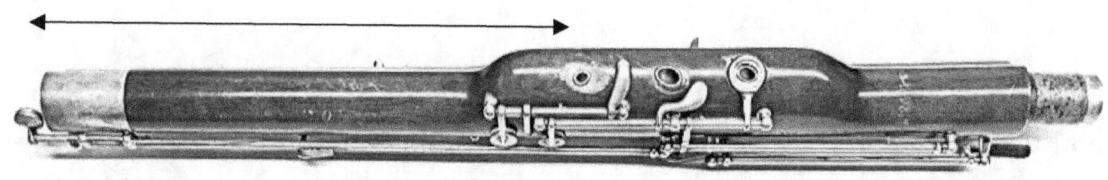

Bassoon Key System

Fingering for the bassoon is more complex than for other woodwind instruments. The following pages are charts showing the bassoon key system, a finger placement chart, and a fingering chart. The average range of a bassoon is from Bb1 to F5. (See Scientific Pitch Notation on page 79.)

Bassoon Key System

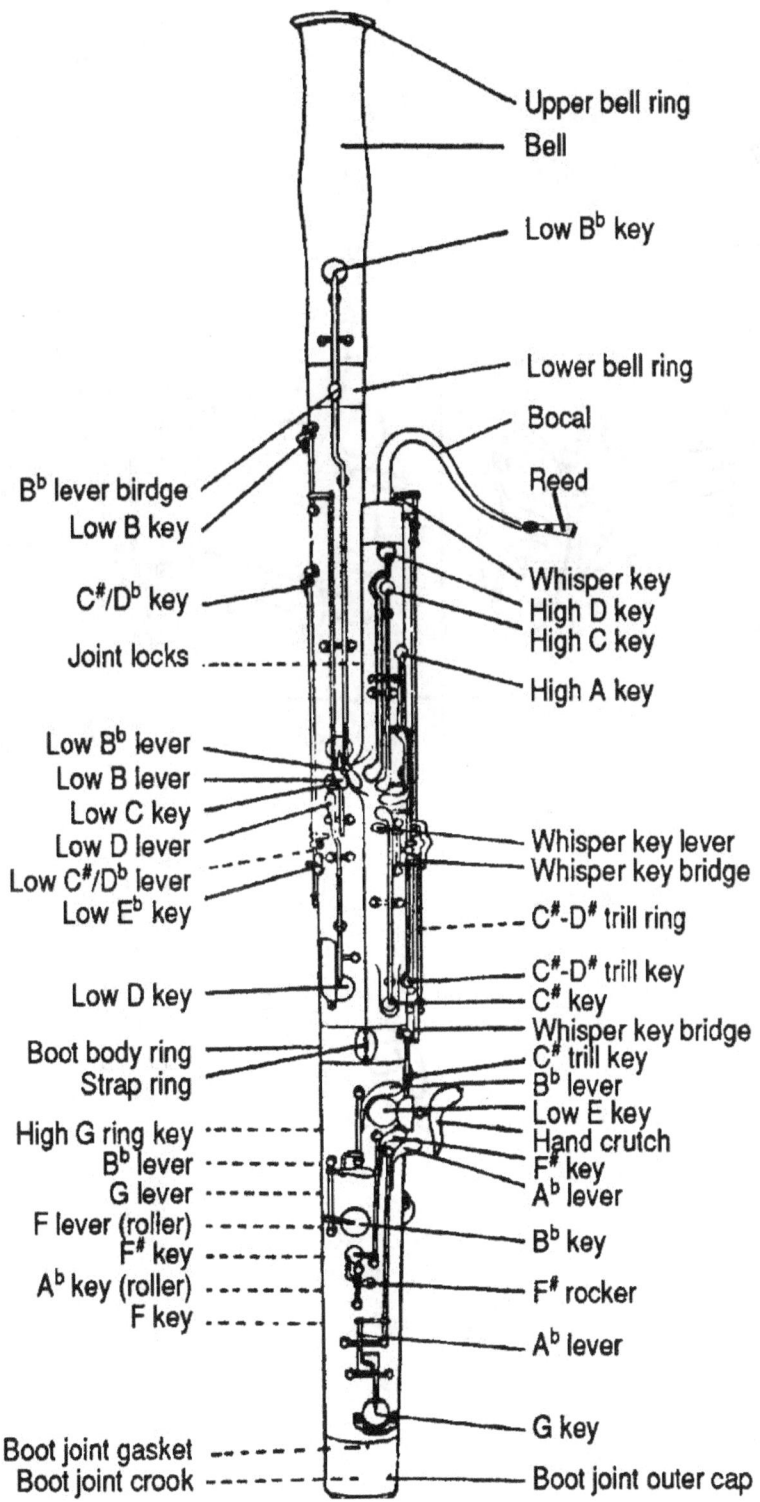

Courtesy of Lawrence Kirmser; The Woodwind Quarterly

Finger Placement Chart

The figure below shows which finger is used on each key.

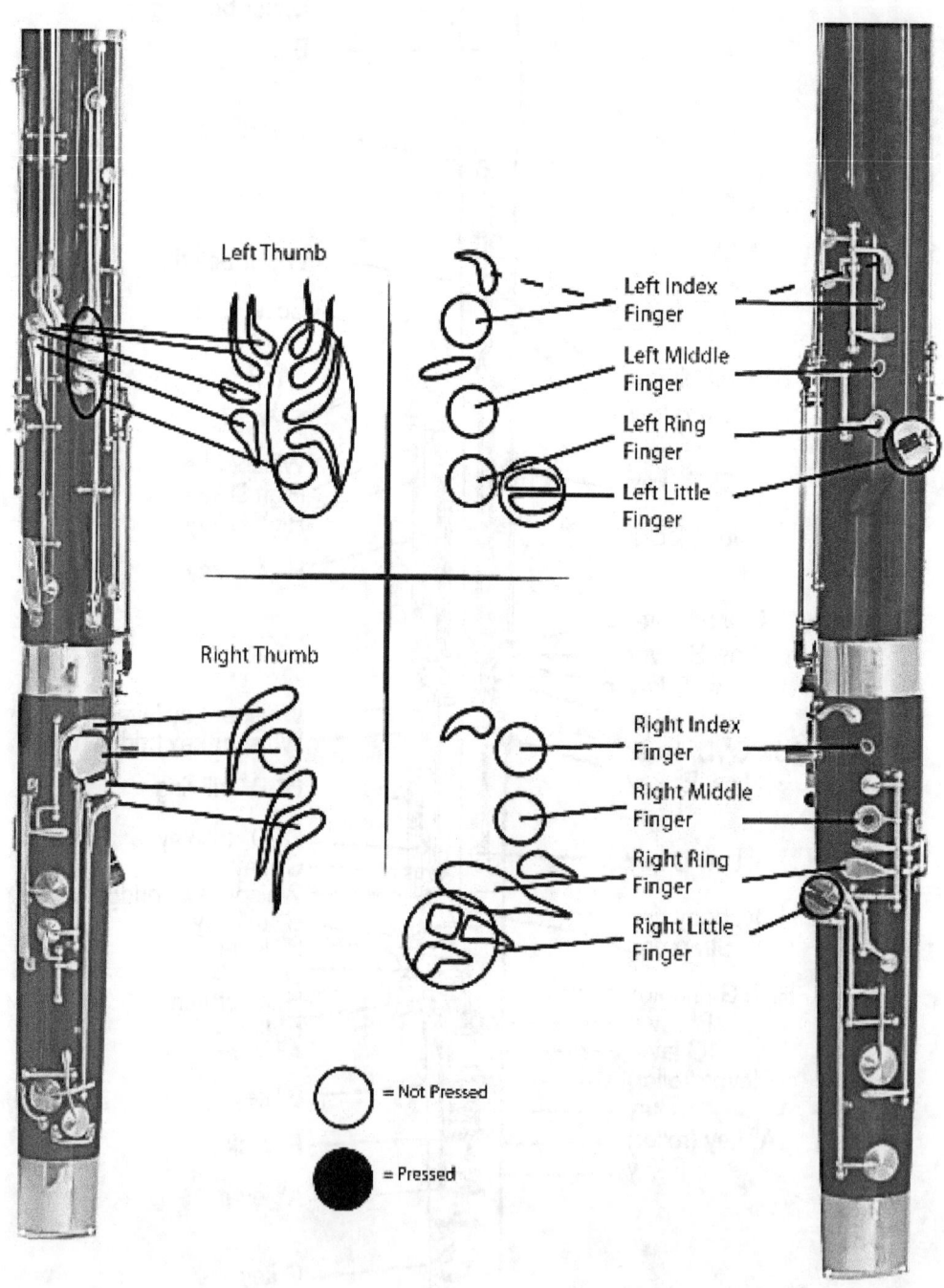

Basic Bassoon Fingering Chart

The figure below shows a basic bassoon fingering Chart. There are some bassoons with slightly different fingerings and keys.

Cover the filled-in tone holes to finger a particular note and depress the filled-in levers below the note shown in the diagram.

Advanced Bassoon Fingering Chart

Courtesy of Woodwind and Brasswind, a Music & Arts company.

In the following fingering chart, all keys on the bassoon are shown in the diagrams under each note. To finger any note, depress the key's levers or cover the tone holes shaded. Special attention should be given to the hole covered by the first finger of the left hand. If the hole's lower half is covered, this one should only be half covered by this finger. A group of important alternative fingerings are included at the end of the chart.

The thumb of the left hand operates nine keys, and the thumb of the right hand operates four keys.

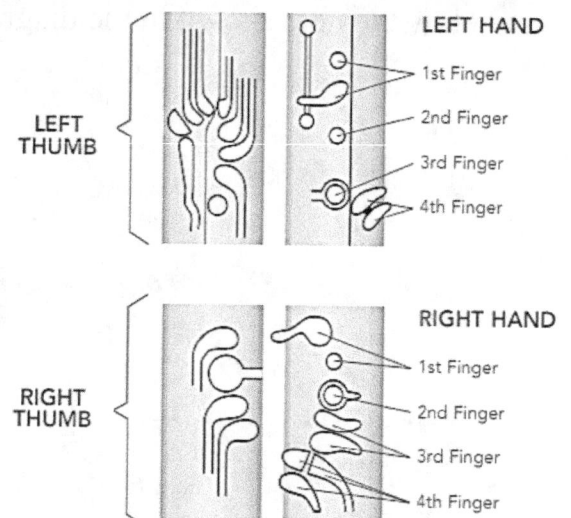

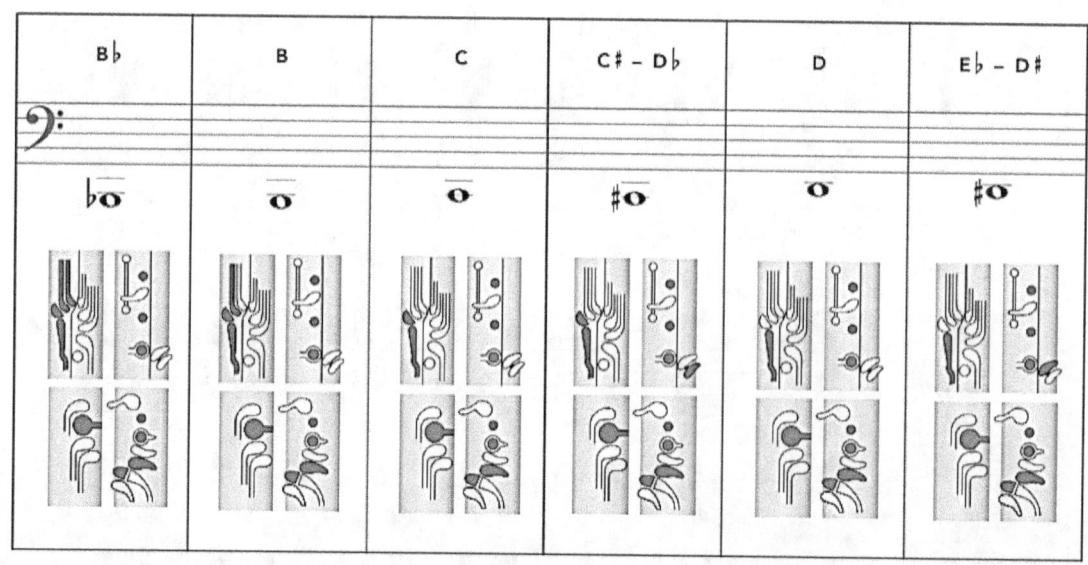

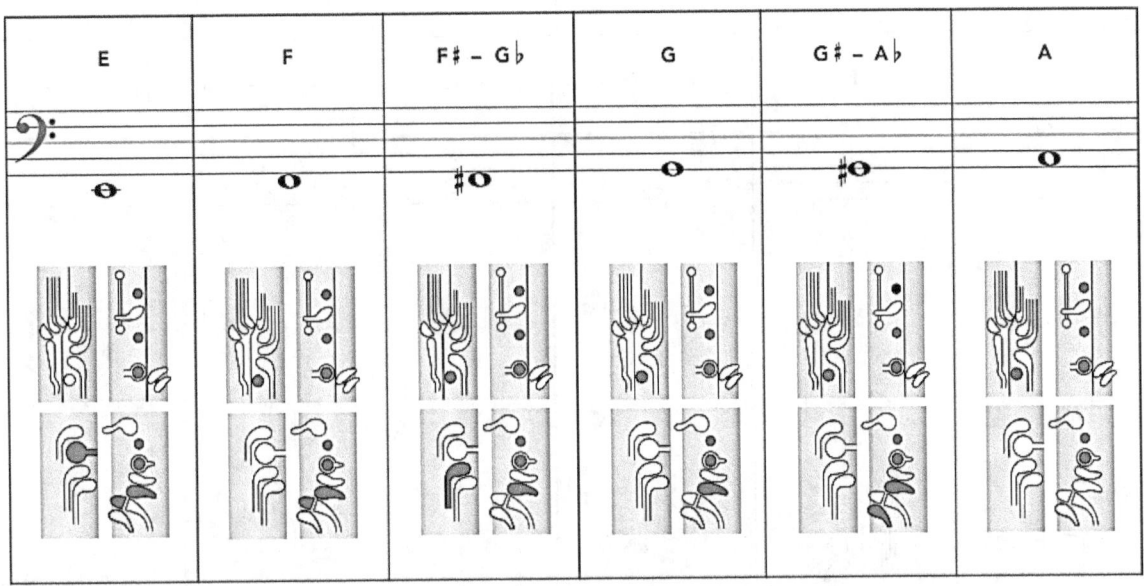
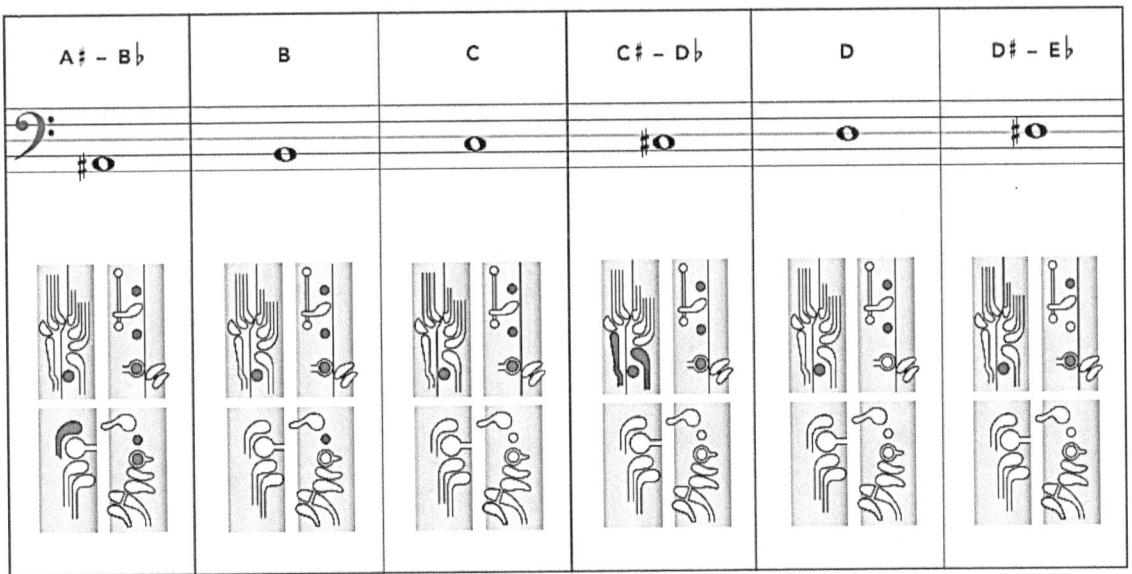

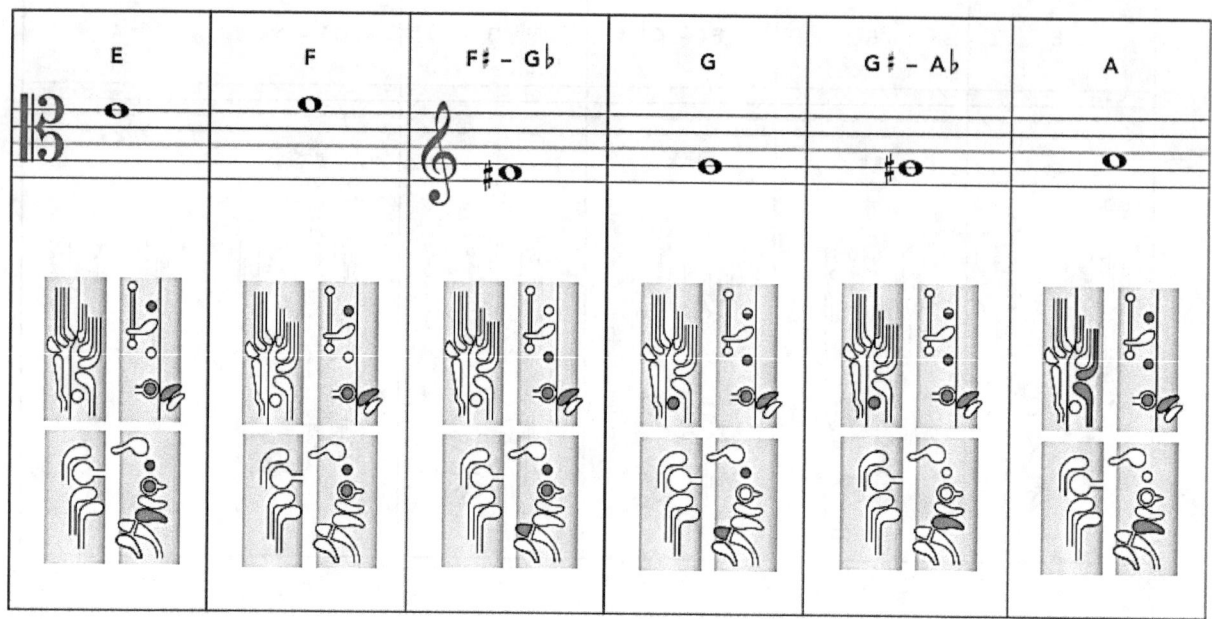
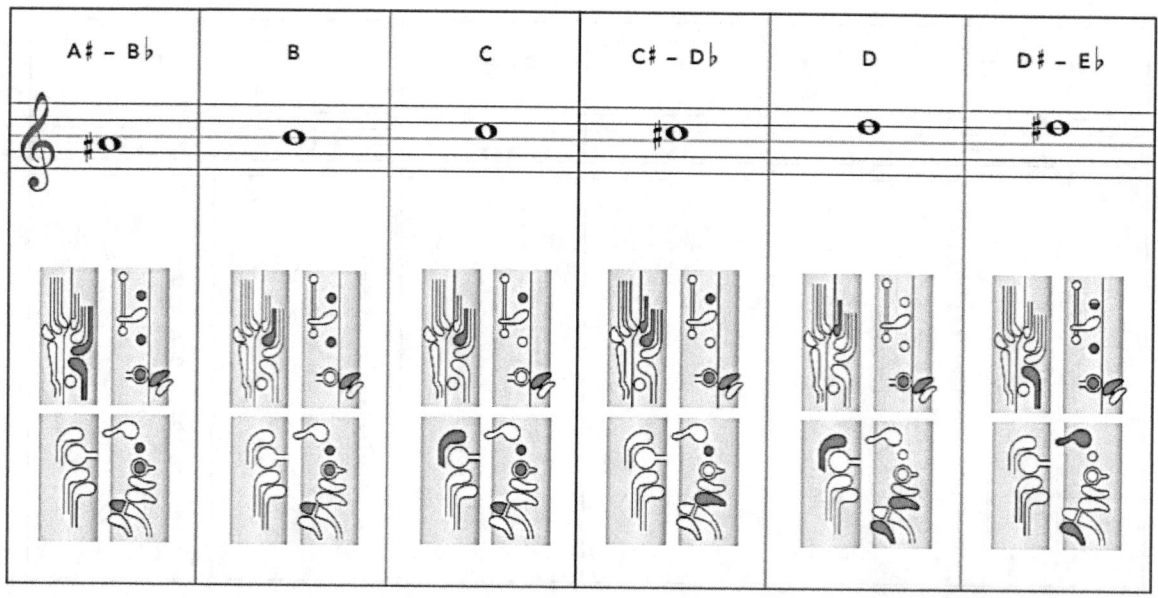

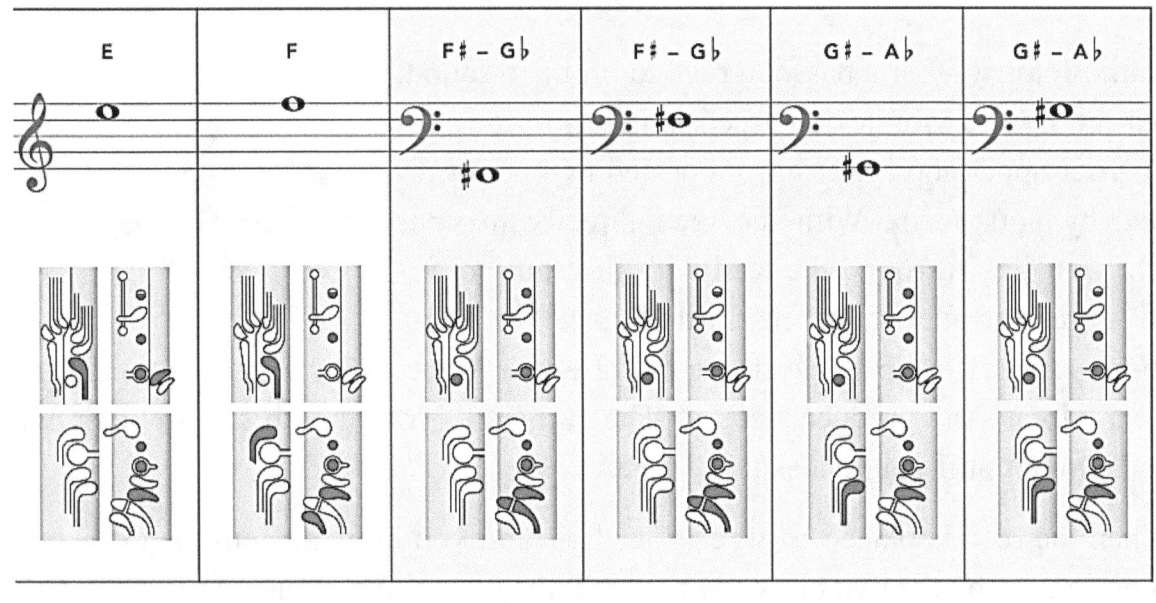

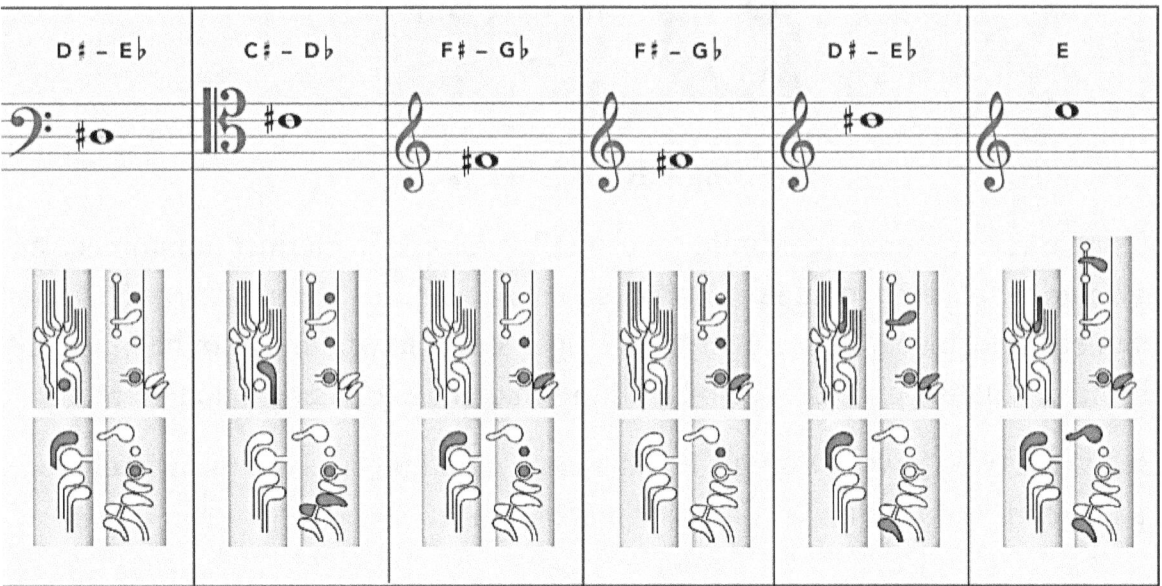

German and French System Bassoons

The German and French systems' two bassoons currently in use look the same. However, there are differences in the number of keys and how they are used. More on this in chapter 3 on different kinds of bassoons.

How Reeds Work

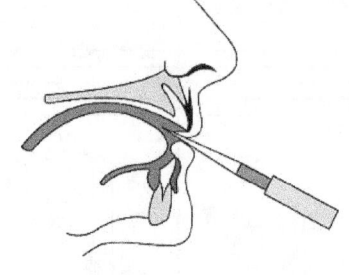

Embouchure—For a bassoon reed to produce sound, it must be free to vibrate. The reed is held in place between your upper and lower lip, supported by but not restricted by your teeth. With the reed directly in your mouth, your lips surround the reed with firm but not restrictive pressure over about one-third of the heart. In this position, your lower lip is the support, while your upper lip is a stabilizer, and the reed can vibrate and produce a sound. The corners of your mouth should be drawn inward. Do not puff your cheeks.

When the reed is placed between your lips, and you blow air into the () shaped opening formed by the two blades of the reed, the blades vibrate against one another to produce a sound.

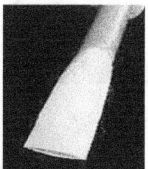 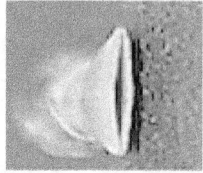

The Single Reed Alternative

A single-reed mouthpiece similar to a small version of a clarinet mouthpiece enables a clarinet player to double on the bassoon in a "pinch." The single-reed bassoon mouthpiece is also very convenient for younger students who may not be musically or physically mature enough to handle all the challenges of using a double-reed.

Below are two views of a single reed bassoon mouthpiece, a clarinet mouthpiece, and a bassoon reed for you to compare them.

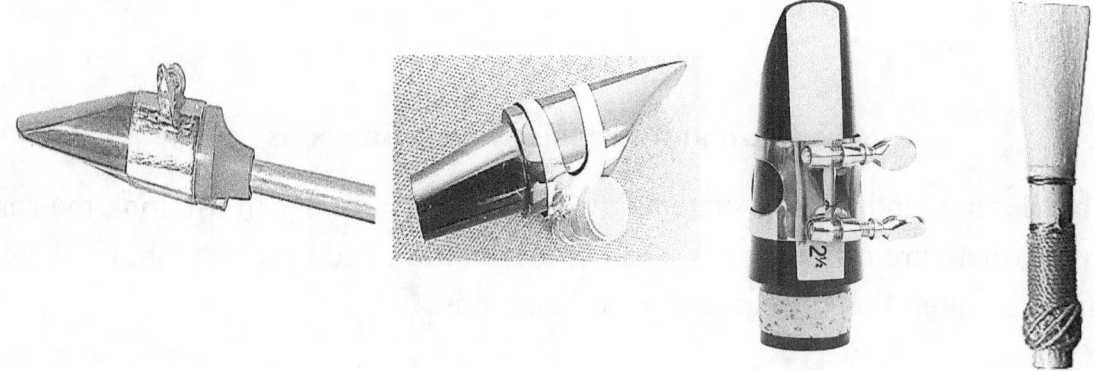

Chapter 3

What Are the Different Kinds of Bassoons?

There have been numerous bassoon-like instruments developed during the past century. Among them are the tenor, tenoroon, and soprano bassoons. These instruments are not commonly in use at this time. You are familiar with the bassoon we all play. Below is a student (modified) model bassoon and bass or contrabassoon. The double bassoon or contrabassoon sounds an octave lower than the bassoon. The instrument is designed not as an extension of the bassoon but as a different instrument.

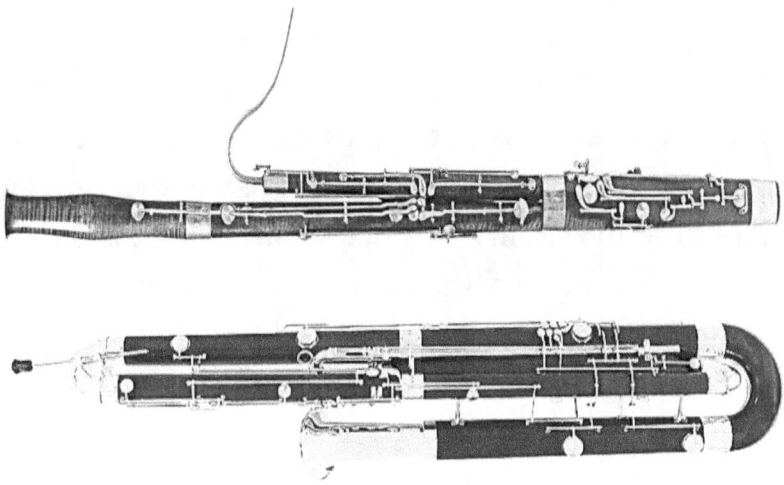

Bassoon and Contrabassoon

Transposition

Before learning about the different bassoons, let's talk about transposition.

A Review of Transposition—You must understand transposition to determine the exact sound your instrument produces from a written note. A non-transposing instrument will sound as written. The written note C will sound like C.

Transposing instruments are referred to as being in a certain key. You will see an Eb piccolo oboe, a Bb trumpet, or an F horn. When the written note C is played on a transposing instrument, the note sounded will be the note in the instrument's name. Playing a written C on a transposing instrument in Bb will sound a Bb.

Why Do Different Bassoons Play in Different Keys?

    To increase the range of an instrument, other versions of the same instrument are made in different sizes. Smaller sizes produce notes in higher ranges, and larger sizes produce notes in lower ranges. This arrangement allows you to play these instruments using almost the same fingering. The result is these become transposing instruments.

    Sarrusophone—A bassoon-like instrument called the sarrusophone appeared in 1856, enjoyed a few decades of popularity, and then faded into relative obscurity until the beginning of the 20th century. At that point, the contra-bass sarrusophone in EEb and CC appeared. These instruments were not exactly popular as entities but were usually assigned by composers to fill unique musical effects within some major works. In addition to being extremely large and unwieldy, sarrusophones produce a timbre that can be described as that of a saxophone at its less refined moments. Presently, sarrusophones are primarily used in wind ensembles and as needed when scored in any major work past and present.

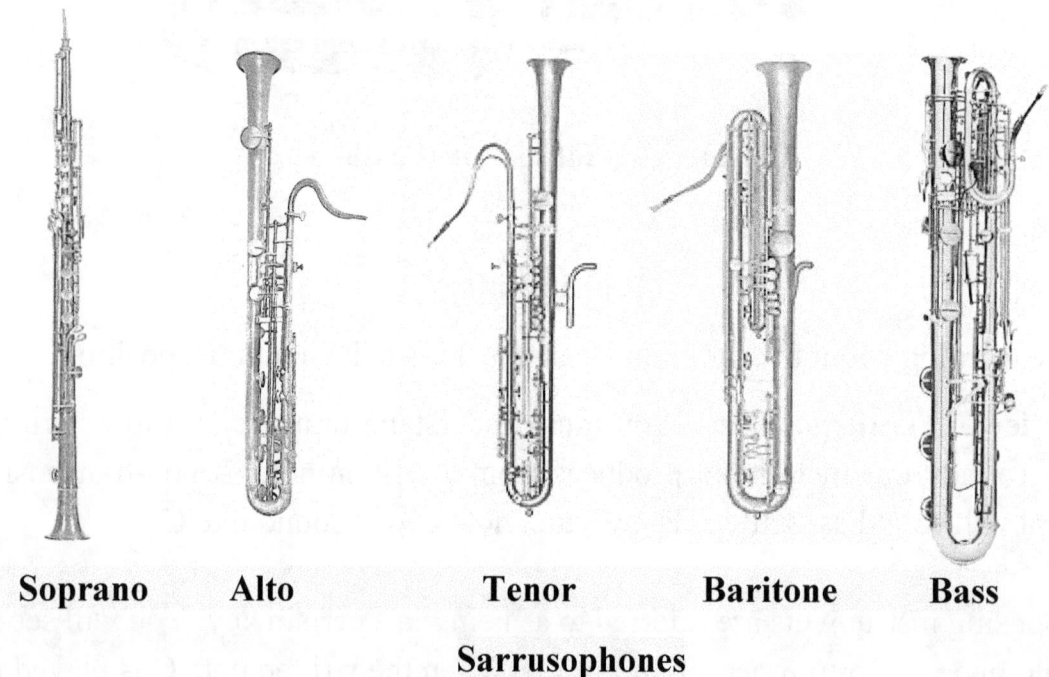

Soprano   Alto   Tenor   Baritone   Bass

Sarrusophones

Complements of the Metropolitan Museum of Art

Heckelphone—Unlike the heckelphone clarinet, the name heckelphone (without the word clarinet) is applied to a four-foot long, bassoon-like double reed instrument that sounds one octave below the oboe and with a slightly extended lower range. The heckelphone has a wider bore than the oboe, producing a fuller, more resonant tone. This instrument provides the lowest third voice of a double reed section combined with an oboe and English horn. The heckelphone is also an acoustic transition between the oboe family instruments and the bassoon.

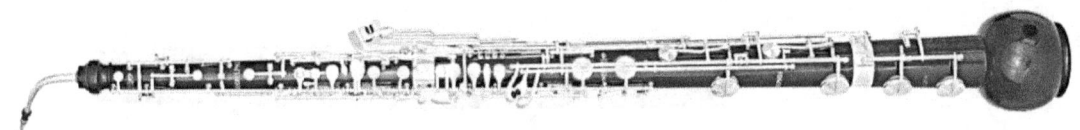

Heckelphone

Bassetto—As instrumental music education has become a nationwide part of the school curriculum, the need for instruments that are easier to handle for young students has motivated manufacturers and instrument designers to create modified versions of the larger instruments. Among these in the double reed lower instrument category is the bassetto, a small bassoon. This instrument is built on the same principles as the traditional bassoon.

The bassetto has a maple body, lined boot and wing joints, and silver-plated keys. The difference between the bassetto and the bassoon is its overall size and a modification of the tone holes to accommodate a more convenient key system. The manufacturer claims the instrument is designed for bassoon students from ages 7–12.

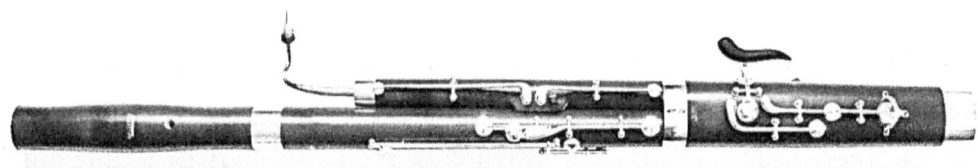

Bassetto

Tenoroon—The tenoroon was also designed to provide younger students the opportunity to experience playing the bassoon. The instrument weighs about 2 ½ pounds instead of a bassoon, which weighs almost eight pounds. The tenoroon has key patterns similar to a traditional bassoon except for being more conveniently designed for small hands. Below is a picture of the front and back of a tenoroon.

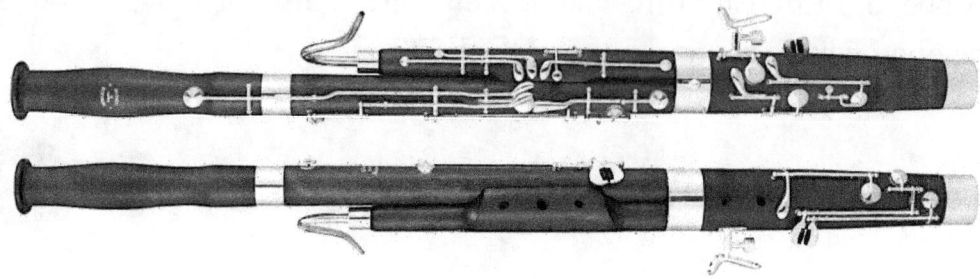

Tenoroon

French and German Key Systems

Two different bassoon key systems are currently used. They are called the German system and the French System. These systems are similar in appearance. However, there are differences in the number of keys, how they are used, and how the keys function is mostly the same as that of the other woodwind instruments.

Padded cups cover holes. The cups are connected and controlled by the player's finger pads. Posts, pivot screws, screw rods and tubes, wire springs, needles, and flat springs are all present in some form, similar to those key systems described in earlier chapters.

Despite all the similarities in design, there remains one great difference between the French and German key systems. The German system bassoon contains many more keys, especially in the boot joint. Specifically, the German system will contain twenty-one to twenty-four keys, depending on the model.

Additional features are assorted rollers for a smooth transition from one key to another, an automatic whisper key, assorted trill keys, ring keys, key guards, joint locks, an extended range, posts and springs that are locked in place with screws, metal-lined tone holes, extra octave keys, and half-hole keys such as those found on the oboe.

All the extras on this rather lengthy list are "extra" only because a bassoon could be played without most of them. They are available on the German model bassoon to ease playing the instrument and improve its intonation and life span. These parts are made of nickel silver or German silver.

The French key system permits the player to perform the same music, but the system is mechanically simpler. It relies more on the player's ability to move from note to note. The French instruments also contain trill keys, finger plates and rings, rollers, and many other devices found in the German design. However, many notes are possible only by using cross fingerings, half-holing (rolling the finger off the hole to cover only half the hole), or trilling certain notes by means other than trill keys specifically designed for that particular trill.

Even though the German system appears to be the system of choice, many European bassoonists still use bassoons built on the French system; American bassoonists almost exclusively use the German system. Below are pictures of the German and French system bassoons.

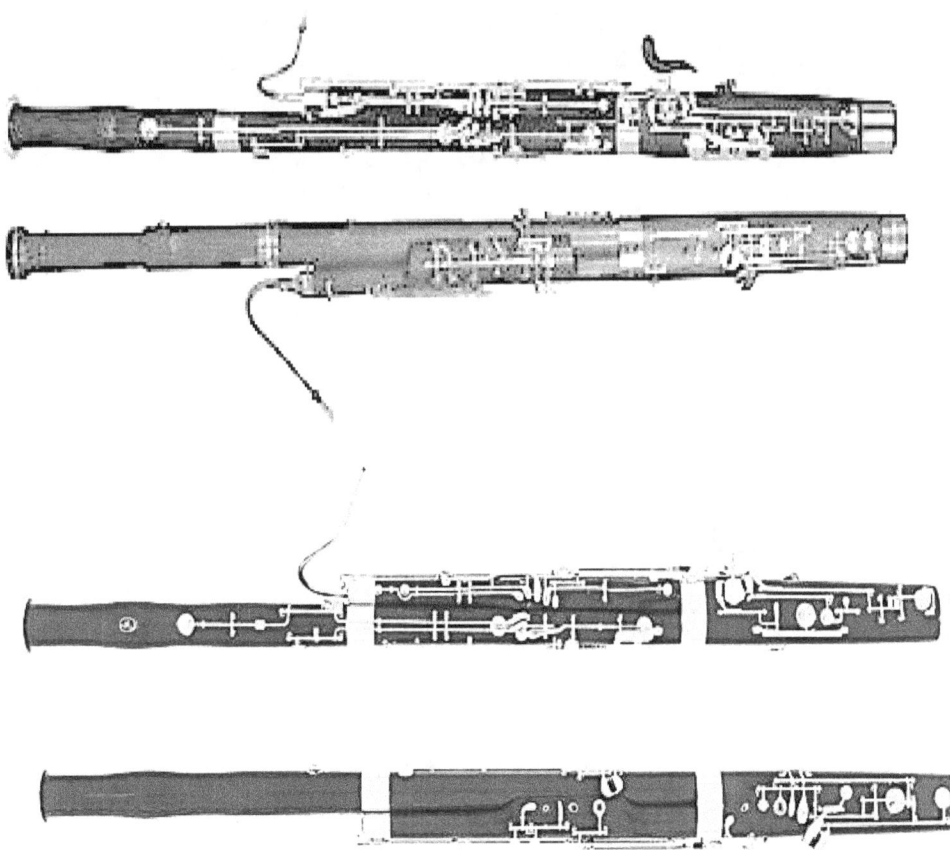

Summary—Bassoon history has provided us with various bassoon-like instruments leading up to the bassoons we now know. The bassoon can be considered the most mechanically complicated woodwind instrument. Unlike other woodwind instruments with standardized key systems (with a few minor exceptions), there are two bassoon models, French and German, with different key systems that sometimes require different fingering to achieve the same notes. In addition to the well-known French and German models, there is a contrabassoon that sounds an octave lower than the other two.

Chapter 4

How Are Bassoons Made?

Bodies—Bassoons are made of maple wood or a plastic composite.

About Wood—Harvested wood is hygroscopic (absorbs moisture) from the environment and, in a sense, continues to live and react to the environment in which it lives. Its structure provides a natural storehouse for moisture, making bassoons react to moisture's harmful and beneficial effects.

When a bassoon is played, the instrument's bore receives warm, moist air from the player's breath. At the same time, the outside of the instrument's body is exposed to the air in the room where the instrument is being played. These two conflicting forces can take their toll on a body made of wood. That being the case, the wood used to make a bassoon must be of the finest quality, properly seasoned, and prepared for its challenging role.

A suitable wood, usually maple for a bassoon, is cut into lengths for the parts to be made. That wood is then dried either in a covered shed in the open air or a kiln, an oven-like device that will dry out the moisture from the wood more quickly than open-air drying.

Kiln Dried Wood

With the wood properly seasoned, the maker refines the cuts to the sizes and shapes needed to make the instrument parts. Those would be the three joints and the bell for a bassoon. At this point, the unfinished pieces called billets are usually rectangles about the size and shape needed for each part.

The shaping process begins after careful inspection to determine which billets will suit each instrument part. The billets are placed on a lathe, shaped, and transformed from rectangles to cylinders.

  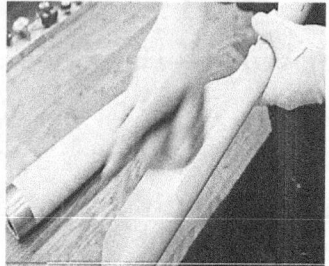

Billet **Shaping the Billet into Cylinders**

The size and shape of an instrument's bore are critical in determining the sound it will produce. The instrument designer makes this calculation and then turns it over to the maker. The bore is drilled into each billet section when dimensions and shape are established.

Drilling a Bassoon Bore

Drilling Tone Holes—When the upper and lower joint body sections are formed and a bore cut into them, drilling the side holes (tone holes) is the next step. The body section is placed in a jig that holds the piece in place under a drill programmed to drill the holes in the locations needed. These tone holes' size, shape, and location are important for the instrument to produce proper pitch and timbre.

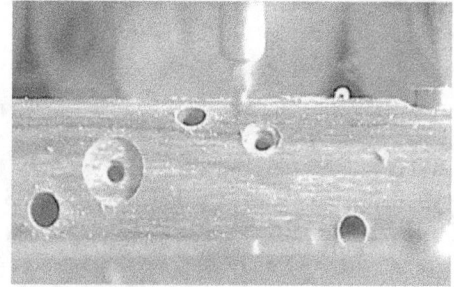

Drilling Tone Holes

Under certain circumstances, a tone hole may be expanded slightly from one end to another (splayed) as it enters the instrument's bore to have proper intonation and pitch. To do this, the craftsperson uses a flaring tool to expand the underside of the tone hole, a process called undercutting.

Undercutting Tone Holes

Along with drilling tone holes, smaller holes are drilled into the body to install the posts that will hold the keys in place.

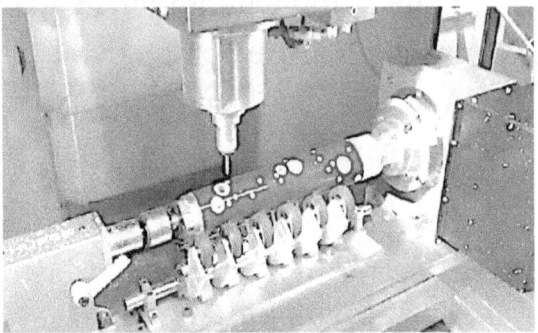

Drilling Post Holes

The tone holes are further refined, and the section is polished. The wooden sections are set to season for another period with this production stage complete.

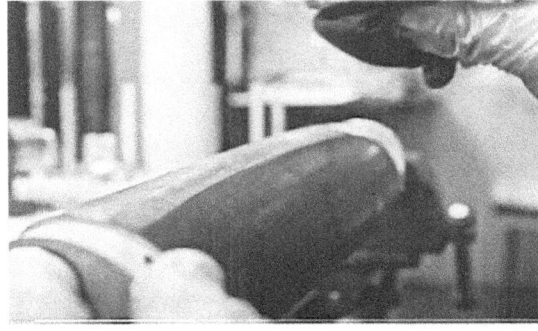

Polishing the Bassoon Body Section

Bassoons are usually made of the hardest selection of maple. Another material that is more durable than wood is bi-thermal reinforced (BTR) Grenadilla. This is a manmade product that combines Grenadilla with ebonite. The result is a product that is crack-resistant, attractive, and a smoother finish for an instrument's bore.

Plastic Bodies—Bassoon bodies can be made of plastic used in injection molding. The plastic granules are heated to a liquid form and injected into a mold that is the shape needed for the instrument part being made. When the plastic cools, it solidifies, and the product is completed.

Resonite—Another product used to make bassoon bodies is called Resonite. This is composed of acrylonitrile butadiene styrene (ABS) and can also be used in injection molding.

Ebonite—Resonite is sometimes confused with ebonite, a hard rubber used to make instrument bodies. Ebonite is formed into billets that can be processed similarly to that used to make a wooden instrument body. These parts are designed by computer-aided drafting (CAD) and made on computerized machinery. With this system, a more precise part can be made in less time and cost than wood-made parts.

Keys—All woodwind instruments have some form of key system. These vary greatly; however, they are made for most woodwind instruments in generally the same way. They can be individually hand-forged by an artisan or mass-produced.

The mass production process begins with making a die for each key. Wax is poured into the die to make a wax mold of the key. The wax key-shaped molds are removed from the die and assembled on a tree-like structure shown below.

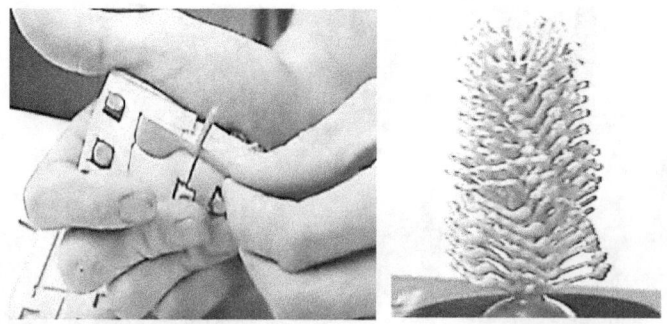

Removing Wax Key from Mold to Make a Key Tree

The tree is placed in a flask filled with plaster that will harden around the tree.

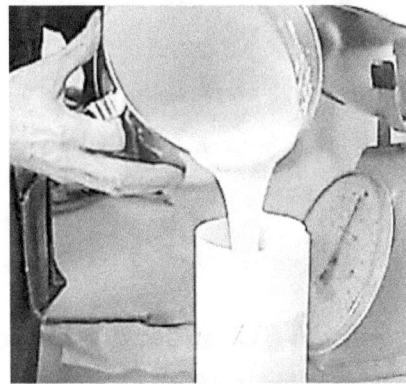

Plaster Cast

After the plaster has hardened around the tree, the wax is melted, and a plaster cast is filled with the molten material used to make the keys. When cooled, the mold is removed, and a tree of metal keys remains. The new key parts are snipped off the tree and soldered together.

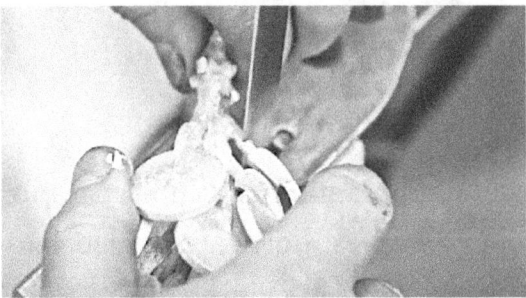

Snipping the Keys off the Tree

To make hand-forged keys, the metal of choice, usually nickel silver, is used to shape individual parts of the key.

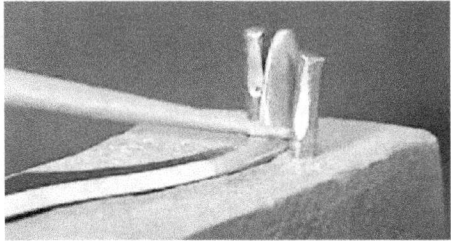

Hand Forged Keys

The hand-forged key parts are soldered together to form a complete key.

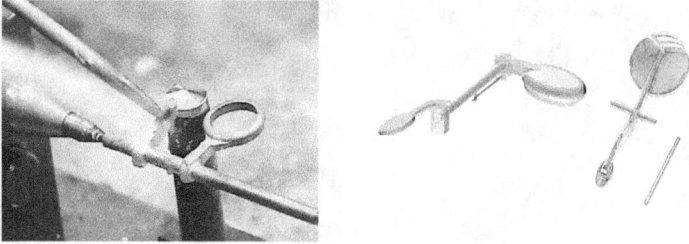

Soldering Hand-Forged Keys

The keys are polished in preparation for assembly on the instrument.

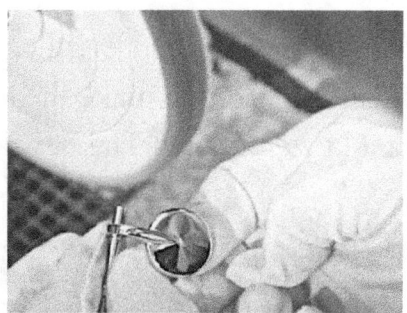

Polishing Keys

Posts are affixed to the instrument's body in preparation for receiving the keys. For instruments with wooden bodies, holes are drilled into the body, and the posts are screwed into those holes.

Drilling Post Holes

For plastic bodies, the posts are often installed by a sonic welding process, which uses high-frequency sound waves to melt the metal posts directly into the plastic.

Sonic Installing Posts

When all the posts are installed, holes are drilled in the posts to prepare for installing the rods and screws that will hold the keys in place.

Wire, needle, or flat springs control the up and down motion of the keys.

Wire   **Needle**   **Flat**

The figure below shows wire springs installed on posts.

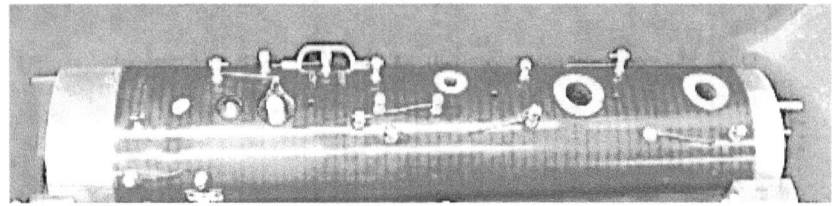

Wire Springs

All bassoons have tenons wrapped with a cork gasket or wrapped with tenon wrapping thread and paraffin. These wrappings hold the joints in place and seal them to prevent leaking.

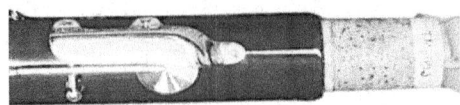  

Cork Wrapped Tenons   **Thread Wrapped Tenon**   **Wrapping Thread**

Pads are glued in the keys, which will cover tone holes.

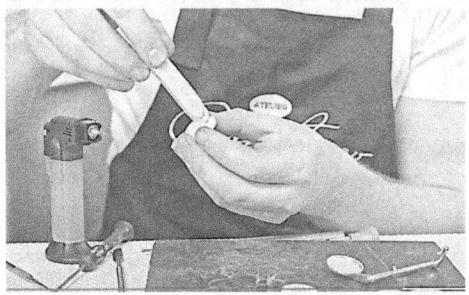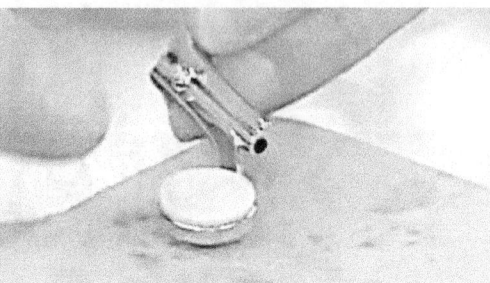

Installing a Pad

When the tenon corks are in place, the keys are installed, springs are placed on hooks, and the screws or rods are connected.

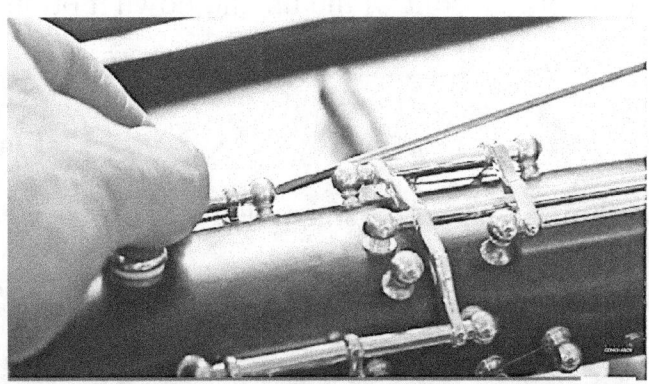

Installing Keys

With the padded keys in place, the bassoon is checked and tested by an expert who performs a set of musical phrases designed to put the instrument through its paces.

Summary—The bassoon is a complicated device requiring many detailed steps to make. The process begins with selecting the material to be used for the body. From then on, the cylinder is shaped, the tone holes are drilled, the bore is polished for wooden models, keys are molded and polished, assembled to the body, and the completed instrument is checked and adjusted.

Chapter 5

How Do I Take Care of My Bassoon?

Bassoons require "per-use" care and more extensive periodic care. The per-use care includes cleaning, swabbing the bocal and bore, lubricating cork tenons, and making minor adjustments. Keeping a bassoon bore swabbed and cleaned after each use is essential to its well-being.

Periodic care includes any major action or repair such as complete cleaning, oiling the bore and exterior body for wooden instruments, cleaning the bore on plastic instruments, cleaning and lubricating tenon corks or thread, and lubricating moving key parts.

Bore Care

Per Use—Take apart your bassoon and clean the bore with an appropriate swab after each use. There are many swabs available, which will be discussed in chapter 8. You must choose the swab that suits you best and is made for your bassoon. You will need three swabs to properly swab your bassoon after each use. An additional brush swab is needed when you proceed to periodic cleaning of your bocal.

Below is a bocal swab, one in action in a bocal, and a bocal brush in and out. See chapter 5 on bore care.

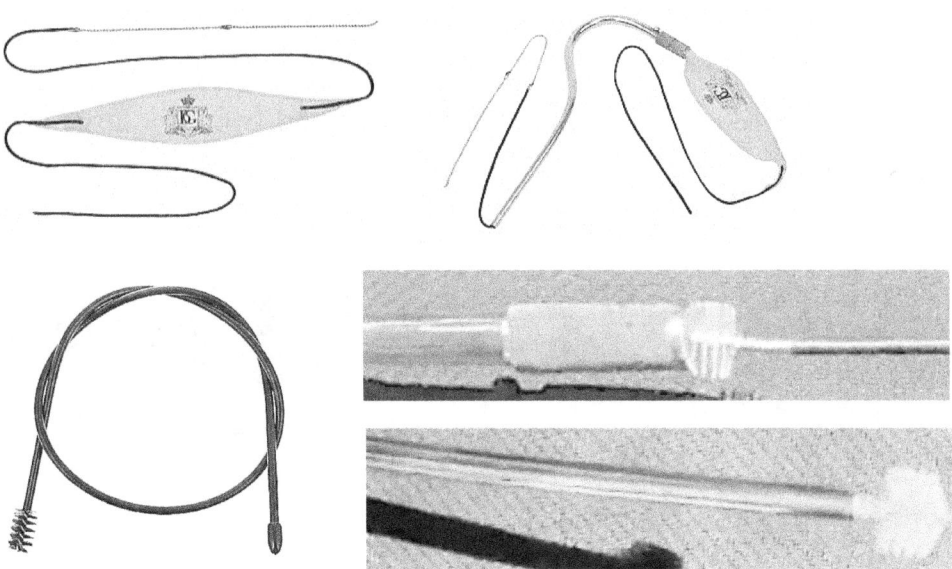

Bocal Swab and Brush

Swabbing the Bocal

The bocal should be swabbed after every use.

1. Rinse the bocal out with warm water if possible.

2. Using a silk bocal swab with a weight on one end, drop the weight through the bocal on the cork side and work it so the weight comes out the other end.

3. Work the swab back and forth as needed.

4. Remove the swab

5. Launder or replace the swab as needed.

6. Wipe the outside of the bocal with a chemically treated silver polishing cloth.

When we discuss periodic cleaning, you will use the same process with a bocal brush pictured above.

Swabbing the Wing Joint

1. Using a weighted microfiber or silk swab designed for a wing joint, drop the weight through the bottom of the joint.

2. Work the weight down so it comes out of the other end of the joint.

3. Work the swab back and forth as needed.

4. Remove the swab.

Below is a picture of a wing joint swab being pulled from the large hole out through the small hole.

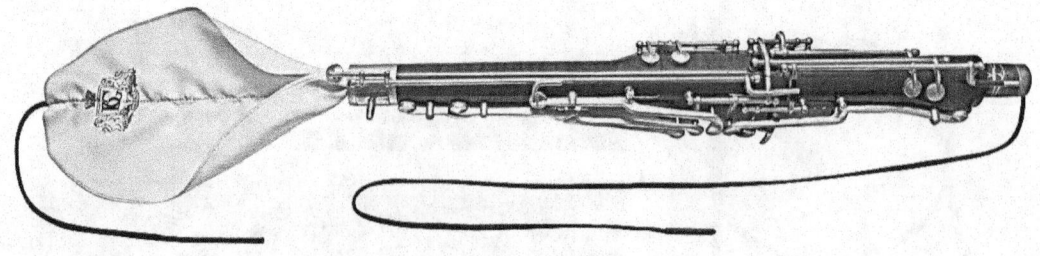

Swabbing the Wing Joint

1. Using a microfiber or silk boot joint swab, drop the weighted end through the larger hole.

2. Turn the joint upside down and work the weight so it comes out of the smaller hole.

3. Work the swab back and forth several times as needed.

4. Check the receiver hole for residual water, and if present, wipe it with the swab cloth.

5. Remove the swab.

Below is a picture of a boot joint swab being pulled from the large hole out through the small hole.

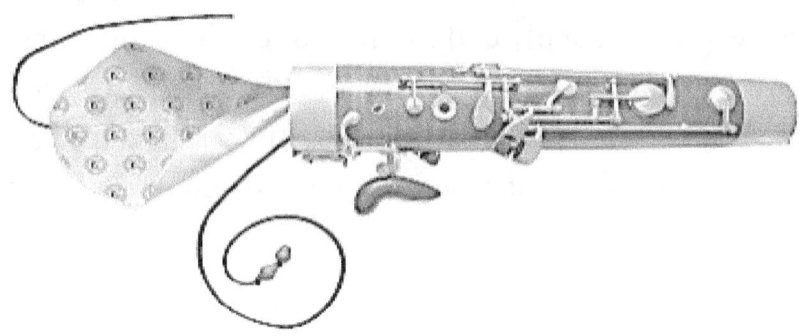

Swabbing the Boot Joint

Because wood absorbs moisture (hygroscopic), it must be protected from extreme temperatures and humidity. When you play your bassoon, you expose the bore to a warm, humid airflow. At the same time, the bassoon body is exposed to the air in the room, which is different from that in the bore. This combination can cause cracking, checking, and, at the very least, surface damage to the bore.

If an instrument with a wooden body is new, it will be wise to "break it in" by limiting your use to short periods several times a day. Breaking in an instrument is important. There are different opinions about how to do it. A safe bet is to play the instrument for 5 to 20 minutes once or twice a day for two weeks and have a backup instrument on hand so you do not overdo playing the new one.

Oiling the Bore

Then, there is the issue of oiling or not oiling the bore. Some say every six months, others say occasionally, and another group says no because it deadens the sound. Ask your teacher or other professional to help you with this decision.

Periodically—Regarding oiling the bore, most new instruments come with the bore oiled. You can check on that from the maker. If it has not been oiled, do so immediately before using the instrument. As mentioned previously, wood is hygroscopic and alive. You should protect the interior of that instrument before it is used.

Since wood continues to live even after it is harvested, it will continue to require a balance of the elements that were part of its existence before it was harvested, namely moisture and oil. These two elements are provided by nature before the wood is harvested; however, that supply ends at the harvest. The moisture then becomes a factor in the environment where the harvested wood will live, and the oil supply must be provided by proper maintenance. The effect of those two conditions on a wooden instrument's body can be easily accommodated by following a few simple procedures.

Never subject an instrument with a wooden body to extreme temperatures or humidity. As you play the instrument, you force warm, humid air onto its inner walls while the outer walls live in whatever the surrounding atmosphere provides. This condition harms the wood's well-being, so you must maintain humidity and natural oil balance within the wood's cells. Perform those tasks, and your instrument will be good for centuries.

Remember, balance is the operative word in this procedure. Too much oil or moisture can be as bad as not enough. Excess oil will prevent the wood from breathing, and too much moisture will set the stage for mildew and fungi growth, ultimately leading to wood rot.

The next consideration is what oil to use. The music industry provides various "bore oils" specifically for bassoon bores. Seek what you feel is the best commercial bore oil on the market. Two well-known brands are oils made by Doctor's Products and Naylors. The choice is yours.

The Process—The best way to oil a bore is to remove all the keys before beginning the process. This allows you to proceed without getting oil on the pads and gives you full access to all instrument parts. I recommend you <u>not do this</u>.

A more realistic alternative is to cover all padded keys with plastic wrap as your first step. Keys can easily be wrapped by slipping the wrap under the pad side of the key and then wrapping the plastic around the metal side. A few minutes doing this job will pay off in avoiding possible aggravation when an oiled pad begins to stick.

When you decide which oil you will use, apply enough oil to the cloth of a weighted pull-through swab to saturate the cloth completely. Wrap the saturated swab cloth in another absorbent cloth and twist them together as if you would wring out a wet rag. The oil from the swab cloth should be absorbed by the secondary cloth, leaving the swab cloth with just the correct amount of oil to begin the job.

When you have determined that the cloth is adequately infused with the proper amount of oil, pass the cloth through the bore of individual sections of the instrument as you would if you were swabbing the instrument after normal use. Repeat this procedure several times.

An hour after all sections of the bore have been treated, and you are sure you have not missed any spots, pass a clean swab through the entire bore to remove any accumulated excess oil. Remove the pad covers and the job is done.

Tenon Care

Bassoons can have either cork-wrapped or thread-wrapped tenons.

For cork-wrapped tenons:

1. wipe the cork on the tenon with a cloth dampened with rubbing alcohol. The cork will appear lighter in color when it is clean.

2. Apply a light coat of cork grease of choice. Always use a light coat. You only need enough to ease a tenon's in-and-out motion. There should be no residual grease visible after the corks are greased.

3. After you apply the cork grease, give those fingers a good scrubbing before you play the instrument, so you do not apply cork grease to the keys.

For thread-wrapped tenons:

Use paraffin wax available in most grocery stores. Rub the wax onto the thread wrapping in the direction of the wrapping. Never rub across the threads. Remember, less is more. Do not use cork grease on thread-wrapped tenons.

Key Maintenance

Per Use—The keys on bassoons require several kinds of care. The parts that come into contact with your fingers should be wiped clean regularly to be determined by your hand hygiene. This is best done with a soft cloth or, for silver-plated keys, with a chemically treated silver polishing cloth. Under no circumstances should any liquid polish be used on keys. It is unnecessary, can harm the keys' motion, and might damage the pads. A wipe with your cloth of choice will do the job.

Periodically—Buy a soft-bristle brush, such as those used for makeup, and brush off the lint and residue that may collect between the keys. If there is any evidence of a substance that the brush will not remove, use a Q-tip to take care of that. Be careful not to displace a spring or damage a pad during this process.

The next issue of importance in key maintenance is lubrication. Depending on use, the age of the instrument, and the environment in which it lives, make a judgment as to how often lubrication is needed, but be flexible since conditions such as climate, use, and locations may change during different periods throughout the year. Common sense without rigidity in decision-making is always the best route to take.

Selecting Key Oil

1. Avoid the more exotic concoctions and try to identify the commercial oil with the best user rating and go with that.

2. If you are a bassoon oil wonk and are inclined to "study the market," you will find opinions such as avoiding light oil and being sure to use light oil.

3. This contradiction exists because light oil evaporates more quickly than oils of a greater viscosity (thickness). Light oil tends to travel down the post to the instrument's body. This is messy if the body is plastic, destructive if the body is wood, will collect dust and lint, and can loosen the adhesive on any cork the oil may contact.

4. Some bassoon players feel that using thicker oils is better. The choice is yours.

To test the oils' viscosity (thickness), turn the bottle up and down to see how the contents moves. The slower the oil moves about, the thicker it is. When you have decided which oils should be considered, place a drop of each, side by side, on one end of a smooth flat surface. Then raise that end of the surface and observe the rate of speed at which the oils travel downward. Thicker oils will move more slowly.

With several choices, try each on one key using a different key for each trial. Do not combine different oils during the trial. Some brands will offer oils in different viscosities appropriate for different instruments. Be sure to use bassoon oil.

The Process—There are many opinions (surprise) on how to apply oil to bassoon keys. Some suggestions are:

1. Use a drop of oil on the tip of a toothpick.

2. Others recommend an eyedropper, which is a bad idea because one drop may be too much oil.

3. A hypodermic needle or some other small, pointed object to move the oil from the bottle to the key.

I recommend you use one of the oil brands that offer an application tip. This oil bottle with an appropriate-sized injection-type needle will dole out the amount needed for an application.

Key oil is needed to prevent rust, quiet the key's action, and lubricate the key's moving parts. To ensure that the oil you use on the keys does not seep onto the instrument's wooden body, I recommend using synthetic oil instead of petroleum-based. Synthetic oils are also less likely to evaporate. Trial and error on your part will eventually allow you to pick a brand that will serve your needs. In the most general sense, you should apply oil sparingly as needed to all moving key parts.

If you look at a key joined to an instrument, you will easily see where that drop of oil should be placed. Keys are held on a bassoon's body by posts through which a pivot screw is inserted to hold the key in place. These screws are connected to the key barrel, a tube on which a pivot screw secures the key from both sides.

The picture below shows two arrows pointing to two places where pivot screws should be oiled. Look through the keys on your bassoon, and you will find many more such connections.

Points to Oil

The actual application of oil is a simple process. "Less is more." The amount of oil and how often it should be used should be minimal. Use the applicator tip to apply the smallest amount of oil possible to both sides of the key barrel at every point where a key that moves is connected to the instrument's posts. Work the key up and down to help the oil travel into the barrel.

You will need to take greater action if a key's operation is sluggish or won't move at all. If that is the case, you will need additional equipment, a flat surface on which to work, and the time and patience to fix the problem.

If you have any mechanical ability, this will be an easy job. If you consider yourself to be a "call the man" type, by all means, bring the instrument to a certified repair person.

To proceed, you will need correct size bassoon screwdrivers, a needle nose plyer, a large absorbent cloth, a smaller absorbent cloth, isopropyl alcohol, pipe cleaners, penetrating oil, and the key oil of choice. You will be working on the soft cloth spread on a flat surface. I find a bath towel is best.

1. Spread the towel out on a flat surface.

2. Place the instrument section to be worked on the towel.

3. Remove all the lint and dust accumulated within the key system using a soft bristle brush.

4. Put a drop of oil on both sides of the barrel of the problem key.

5. Work the key up and down until it moves more easily than it did previously.

6. Loosen and then retighten the screw.

Should the screw be rusted or bound in place, use a single drop of penetrating oil at the contact points. Let the penetrating oil remain for 15 minutes while you work the key up and down periodically. Make every effort not to get the penetrating oil on the instrument's body.

When you feel enough time has passed, try to _tighten_ the screw the tiniest bit to break the bind. Then try again to loosen the screw. During this process, you must use a screwdriver that is a perfect fit for that screw slot to help prevent stripping the screw. If you cannot move the screw, bring it to a professional.

7. If you are removing a pivot screw, it should come out easily. If it is a rod screw after the thread clicks, indicating it is unscrewed, remove the screw with the needle nose plyer. The key will come out of place, but it is easy to replace after the screw is cleaned.

8. Clean the rod screw with alcohol on the small rag.

9. Pass an alcohol-moistened pipe cleaner through the key's barrel.

10. Pass an oil-moistened pipe cleaner through the key's barrel.

11. Return the key to its original position and replace the screw.

If you find rust on the key springs during this process, use a Q-tip to swab the affected spring with some oil.

Sticking Pads—The best solution to sticking pads is preventing them from happening. If you, as the player, avoid any food or drink other than water one hour before playing your instrument, the likelihood of your pads' sticking will greatly diminish.

When you eat or drink, other than water, your breath carries tiny particles of food and vapors that contain anything in your mouth at the time, through your instrument and onto its pads. If you do not eat or drink, there is still some small chance of sticking pads caused by the moisture that the pads will inevitably pick up, combined with dust and residues of any kind in the environment.

Another cause of sticking pads can be any bore or key oil seepage that might migrate to the tone hole edges and then to the pads. To avoid this situation, you must follow the "less is more" rule when applying oil to your instrument.

Treatment —Before treating a sticking pad, be sure a weak spring is not the cause of the problem. Bending the spring slightly in the same direction it already takes can make a significant difference. If that does not help, proceed with the pad cleaning process.

Holding the instrument with the offending key located next to your ear, work the key. If the pad is sticky, you will hear a subtle clicking sound showing the pad sticking to the tone hole. If that sound is present, move on to treating the pad. There are several approaches to treating a sticking pad.

If the pad is old or showing signs of wear, the best solution is removing the key, cleaning the tone hole edge with a bit of bore oil for a wooden instrument or alcohol for plastic, and replacing the pad with a new one.

If the pad is in good condition and the tone hole edge is clean, you might want to try some of the remedies on the market. There are various pad cleaning papers that you can place between the offending key and its tone hole. Close the key gently on to the paper and withdraw the paper.

Another option is using keypad powders, which are supposed to remedy the sticky pad problem when applied to the pad.

Some technicians recommend swabbing the pad with a Q-tip moistened in lighter fluid. Others suggest the same process using isopropyl alcohol.

The opponents of these methods claim that the paper products will damage the pads, the powders will build up on the pad and worsen the problem, and the lighter fluid is dangerous and can dry out the pads.

A sticky pad is not the end of the world. Over the years, I have used these procedures and found they all work depending on the severity of the condition. You will have to decide by trial and error.

Summary—Bassoon maintenance is the most labor-intensive of all instruments because of their numerous parts, mechanical complexity, and instability of wooden bodies. You will find that the opinions on how these instruments should be maintained are numerous, in many cases contradictory, and at best not supported by convincing empirical evidence to which you can turn.

Your best direction would be to evaluate your situation in terms of your instrument's requirements, how often and where it is used, where and for how long it is stored without use, the climate in which you live, and whatever directions were included with the original packaging if the instrument was purchased new.

Trial and error in selecting the products will eventually bring you to suitable equipment and materials for your situation. As a rule, move thoughtfully, slowly, and intelligently and remember that less is more.

NOTES

Chapter 6

How Should I Plan My Practice Sessions?

You have heard the old saying that "practice makes perfect." Well, practice can make perfect, but only if you practice with understanding, patience, and the will to "get it right."

Playing an exercise or musical selection often will make it better only if you understand how the piece should sound and know how to make it sound that way. Playing a piece incorrectly repeatedly can result in your learning to play it wrong well. Here are some suggestions that will help you get the best results from your practice period:

1. Select a place in your home where you can practice without disturbing your family and where their daily life will not distract you from your work.

2. Pick a practice time that comfortably fits your daily study schedule. Try to use that same time each day.

3. Set a long-term general goal. Then set some short-term goals that will help you reach the long-term goal. Choose a topic like tone quality, intonation, phrasing, and dexterity (moving your fingers fast) as some of these short-term goals. Then apply them to your long-term goal of making beautiful music beautifully.

4. Have a plan for each practice period. What part of your long-term goal do you want to accomplish in each period? For example, "Today, I will work on tone quality and embouchure."

5. How long and how often should you practice? Daily practice is best. However, how long you practice should vary with your short-term goal. Shorter daily practice periods produce better results than less frequent long sessions.

6. After you have set your goal and begun to practice, decide on the amount of time and how often you will need to practice to achieve each target.

7. Discuss your plans with your teacher, who can help you make the plan and reach your goal.

8. Equipment—You must have all the necessary equipment for a successful practice session. Your equipment should include a music stand, metronome, chair if you plan to sit, cleaning cloth, swab, and whatever else you need to be comfortable.

Breathing—Before you continue planning your practice sessions, let's think about your breath, which is the source of the sound you will be making on your bassoon.

A muscle that separates your lungs from your stomach area controls your normal breathing process. This muscle is called a diaphragm. As you breathe, your diaphragm moves up and down. When it moves down, it increases the area in your lung cavity, causing a vacuum that your lungs fill by drawing in air. When the diaphragm moves up, the lung cavity is smaller, and the air in your lungs is pushed out. You can see a great animated example of diaphragmatic breathing on Wikipedia. Search diaphragmatic breathing and look at the right-hand side of the first page for the diagram.

As a bassoon player, one of the most important skills you must master is controlling your diaphragm and, in so doing, controlling your airflow, which is the fuel supply for the tone you produce on your bassoon. Your diaphragm is regulated by your ABS (abdominal muscles). Expanding and contracting those muscles allows you to move your diaphragm up or down.

Try this! Lie down on a flat surface and relax. Place a book on your abdomen and breathe in and out. As you do so, you will notice that the book on your abdomen rises and falls as you breathe. When you breathe in, the book will rise; as you breathe out, the book will fall.

Now, breathe out all the air in your lungs by contracting your ABS. Then, take a deep breath in by expanding your ABS. Do not move any other body part, such as raising your shoulders or expanding your chest. Raising your shoulders does nothing; your chest will expand as your lungs fill with air. This conscious expansion and contraction of your abdominal muscles are called diaphragmatic breathing. It is something you do all day long without thinking about it.

To apply this procedure to play the bassoon, you must take a deep breath by expanding your diaphragm as much as possible. Remember not to expand your chest or raise your shoulders. Your lungs should be full of air. Now let the air out through pursed lips or play a long tone on your bassoon. As you run out of air, give an extra push on your ABS, and you will notice that there will still be a bit more air left to use. Practice this process regularly to develop breath control. The better you control your airflow through "conscious diaphragmatic breathing," the greater the fuel supply you will have for your embouchure.

The Process—Use the following ideas to make your practice period productive.

1. Warm up with some simple scales using long tones that start very softly (pianissimo—*ppp*), increase in volume (crescendo) to a full sound (forte—*fff*), and then gradually diminish the sound (diminuendo or dim.) back to the original *ppp*. Listen as you play. Are you playing in tune and with the best tone quality you can produce?

2. After warming up with some long tones, add your own rhythmic patterns to those same scales. Listen carefully to intonation as you play. Playing in tune is a must for any bassoonist.

3. You can expand the warmup material to include exercises as you advance.

4. Follow your warmup by playing a tune that you like. Enjoy the music.

5. Improvisation is fun. Make up a tune or try to play a tune "by ear." No need for printed music here.

6. Start practicing the material your teacher assigned in your last lesson. Follow the instructions carefully. Listen to yourself, sing the music before you play it, feel the rhythm, and be sure you are playing in tune.

7. Record yourself on your cell phone as you play. Then, listen to the recording and be critical of your intonation, phrasing, and general musicianship.

8. Did you like what you heard? If your answer is yes—great! If it is not, think of what you did not like. Figure out how you can make it better. Then, make it better. Check again to be sure you are playing in tune, using proper embouchure and phrasing. Are you keeping a proper playing position?

Apps and Your Cell Phone—Using your cell phone or computer, you can search for "Apps for bassoon practice." You will find many that are free and will help you practice better. Some sites also have free music that you can print. Others show playing techniques and play-a-long sessions where you join others to play bassoon music. Use the same search on YouTube to find many sites you will enjoy watching while learning about playing and caring for your bassoon.

Summary—Developing a structure for your practice sessions that works for you will increase your level of achievement. Playing "stuff" without a plan may be fun but does not encourage learning. If you are building a brick wall, you must begin with a solid foundation on which that will rest. Your practice periods are the foundation upon which your performance will rest.

Chapter 7

A Survey of the History of Woodwind Instruments

The Flute—The flute results from 43,000 years of history. It probably all began in Slovenia, a European country bordering Italy. In Slovenia, a cave bear's femur (thighbone) carved to look like a primitive flute with several tone holes was discovered. Another instrument made from a vulture's wing bone was found in Germany. That instrument is estimated to be about 35,000 years old. These and other objects tell us that very early on, humankind was becoming aware that a stream of air passing through a tube could produce sound.

Simple flute-like instruments dating back to the pre-Christian era have been discovered in numerous countries. Instruments made from crane bones dated 9000 years old and others made of bamboo from 433 B.C. were discovered in China. Below are some examples of primitive wind instruments. Search Google Images Primitive Flutes to see many other examples.

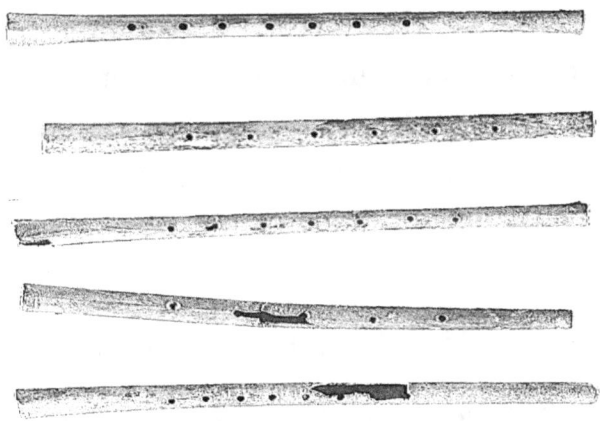

Below is a picture of today's modern flute. Quite a difference!

In 2004, an instrument made from a mammoth tusk and two similar instruments made from swan bones were discovered in southern Germany. Similar instruments have been found in many locations throughout the world. This tells us that there is no absolute way to assign an accurate time or location to the "invention" of the flute.

We must be satisfied with the theory that the flute evolved along with the development of humankind.

By the sixteenth century, the flute had been developed into a one-piece cylinder with six tone holes. Covering the holes with the fingers allows the player to produce different notes within a limited range. To compensate for that limitation, the instruments were made in different sizes, producing different pitches. Larger instruments produced lower sounds, while smaller instruments produced higher sounds. That progress reached a point in the eighteenth century when flute makers began to develop key systems. As a result, we now enjoy the flute we use today.

Jacques-Martin Hotteterre (1674–1763), renowned flutist and instrument maker of the time, is credited with improving the transverse flute by devising the three-piece design with a separate head joint, body, and foot joint structure. From that period on through the early eighteen-hundreds, improvements were made by relocating and resizing the six-tone holes and adding keys. This all resulted in improved intonation and a greater capability to perform chromatics.

Theobald Boehm (1794–1881), In the early 1800s, Boehm, a jeweler, and goldsmith, an accomplished flutist and flute maker, determined that larger, properly spaced tone holes would produce a better tone quality and improved intonation. For approximately twenty years, he redesigned the instrument producing a key system on a three-piece cylindrical body that, with modifications, became the instrument we know today.

The Following Is a Timeline for the Evolution of the Flute.

1000–1400—The Medieval period in world history. The beginnings of society as we now know it.

Below is a reproduction of an instrument that was called a flute during the years 1000 through 1400. Look at the end of the instrument, and you will see no embouchure hole like the one on a flute. In its place is a cut in the wood, which makes a sharp edge (arrow) against which the air blown into the instrument strikes and produces a sound. This type of sound-maker is called a fipple.

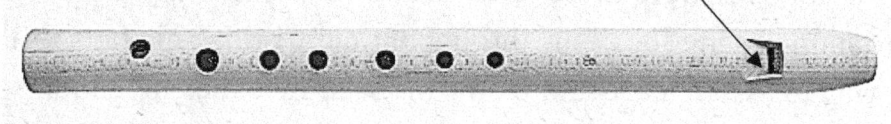

Compare the fipple to the flute embouchure hole pictured below.

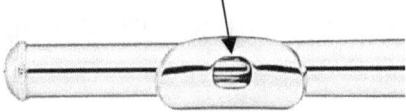

A flute player must direct a stream of air against the edge (arrow) of the flute's embouchure hole. In a fipple instrument, the air stream is directed for you to the exact spot. You might be familiar with a recorder instrument pictured below. A recorder is a fipple instrument.

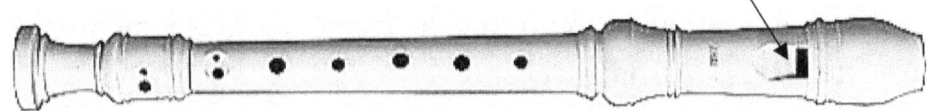

The early instruments, called flutes, had no keys and six equally spaced tone holes. We now name these fipple instruments recorders.

1400–1600—The Renaissance Period in World History. It was a period of reawakening where society began to understand art, science, and music.

Adding an embouchure hole and spacing the tone holes in two sets of three was the next step in developing the flute and oboe. These instruments had a better-sounding upper register but were still not great in the lower notes.

1600–1760—The Baroque Period in World History. It was a period when music, art, architecture, and the general style of living became very elaborate and highly crafted. Much music was written with several complicated, layered melodies at the same time. This is called counterpoint.

During these years, the flute was divided into three and four sections. The bore (inside tube) was tapered, larger at the embouchure hole, and gradually smaller toward the end. With these adjustments, the flute sound improved and could be tuned.

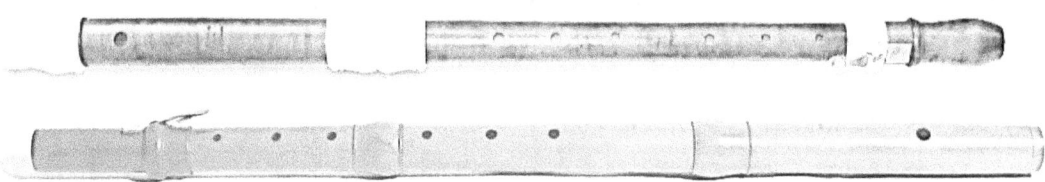

1760–1820—The Classical Period in World History. A period when music and the arts became simpler and music was written with a single melody and harmony (chords).

George Catlin (1778–1852), a musical instrument maker, made a variety of experimental flutes, beginning with one key and gradually adding keys. These additional keys improved the intonation of the instruments and made it possible for a flute player to play more notes with greater ease.

Rick Wilson's Historical Flute Page http://www.oldflutes.com/boehm.htm is a great source of information on the flute's history. Below is a picture of two early Boehm flutes from Rick Wilson's website.

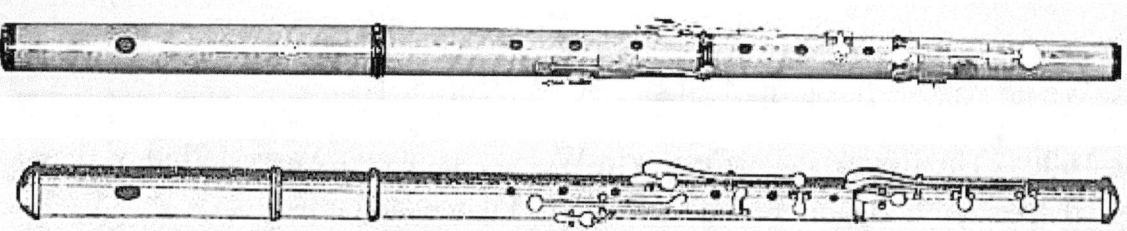

Rick Wilson indicates that these photos and essays may be copied for personal use or used in moderation on web pages, etc., as long as he is clearly acknowledged as the source. All but minimal use of the photos or essays on the web should be accompanied by a link to these pages.

The following is a survey of the history of the other most popular woodwind instruments now in use: the clarinet, saxophone, oboe, and bassoon. You will read about instruments that preceded those, some by several thousand years. Other instruments invented at a known time in music history will receive a more accurate account of their development.

The aulos is perhaps the flute-like instrument most frequently represented in ancient Greek illustrations, literature, and the Bible. Dating as far back as the sixth century B.C., the aulos was used as an accompaniment to vocal performers and as a solo instrument. The primary settings for their use extended to festive occasions of all kinds, athletic events, and funerals. Originally made of various kinds of wood, such as cane or boxwood, more sophisticated bronze, bone, and ivory models appeared.

One version of the aulos was constructed with two pipes, each with a double reed as its sound generator. Different illustrations show the instrument as two units held individually while being played simultaneously. Variations of the aulos will have five to seven tone holes on each pipe and more advanced models with a ring-type device at the top of the pipes. This was used to alter the pitch.

In 1921, twenty-three feet of tubing and assorted fragments were discovered in the tomb of Queen Amanishakheto in Meroe, Sudan. These are believed to be sections of different types of auloi that were parts of a professional musician's equipment.

Aulos

Windcap Instruments

Using a windcap instrument, the player blew through a hole in the top of the windcap and, in so doing, activated the double reed inside. The disadvantage of a windcap sound generator is the player's lack of control over the action of the reed other than to start, increase, or decrease volume to some degree and to stop the sound. All the nuances of pitch, volume, and timbre associated with a player's contact with a reed are lost in a windcap instrument.

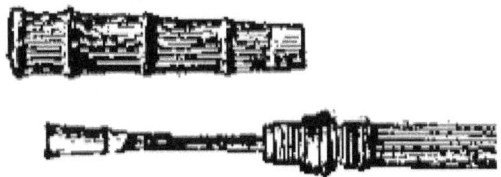

Windcap

The Zummara —The zummara, native to Egypt, had a windcap sound generator. The instrument had two pipes, one functioning as a drone supplying a continuous underlying tone. The other pipe was used to play the melody. The player was required to finger both pipes by spanning the holes on each pipe simultaneously. The intonation was dreadful.

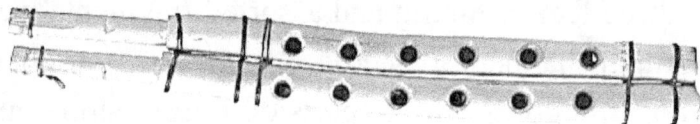

Zummara

The Crumhorn—The crumhorn (curved horn) appeared in Germany in the late fourteenth century and maintained its popularity in Germany, Italy, and the surrounding areas for about three centuries. As a windcap instrument, the player blew through a hole in the top of the windcap and, in so doing, activated the double reed inside.

The crumhorn was constructed with a cylindrical bore similar to a clarinet. This resulted in the instrument's overblowing (raising the register) at the twelfth instead of an octave at which a conical bore instrument would sound. The crumhorn had fingering like the clarinet's chalumeau (lowest) register but was limited to about an octave. The instrument was difficult to play in the upper range, had a somewhat raucous sound, and did not excel in pitch accuracy.

Below is a picture of a crumhorn and a breakdown of its windcap reed unit.

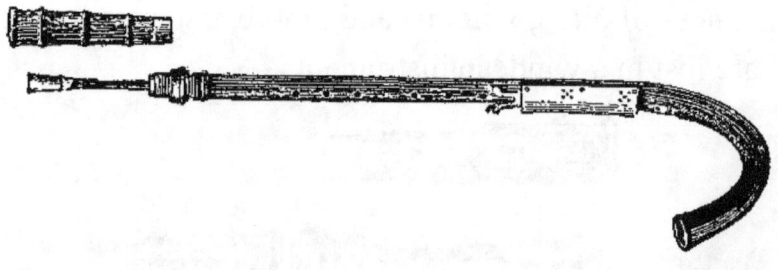

Crumhorn

Single Reed Instruments

Single-reed instruments of the **idioglot** version, where the reed is carved from part of the instrument, date back to three thousand B.C.

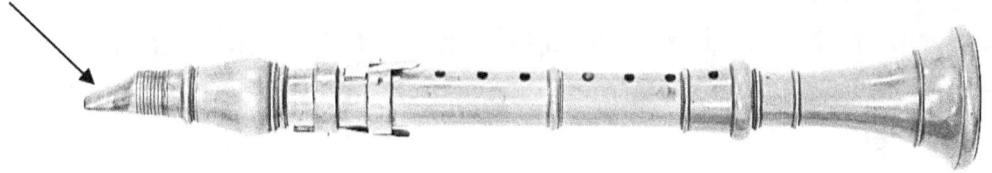

We might speculate that these instruments were the precursors of the clarinet and saxophone.

The Chalumeau—Chalumeau (chalumeaux plural) was used throughout central Europe as early as the twelfth century. The early chalumeau lacked musical sophistication in intonation and tone quality, so its use and repertoire were relegated to folk rather than classical compositions.

Eventually, improvements were made to the instrument so that by 1700 the chalumeau evolved into a single reed woodwind instrument with six tone holes, one key on the front, and one hole on the back. Its range, from F3 below middle C to A4 above middle C, was equal to that of the present-day clarinet's lower so-called chalumeau register. This more sophisticated chalumeau gained acceptance throughout France and Germany and became part of the popular instrumentation.

Chalumeau

Because the chalumeau had a range of only twelve notes, the players were required to use as many as four different models to cover the range from F3, a fifth below middle C, to Bb5 above the treble staff. At this time, eight original chalumeaux are in existence. These are models for contemporary makers who produce chalumeaux to satisfy the present market.

The Clarinet

John Christoph Denner (1655–1707), an instrument maker, along with his son Jacob, is credited with advancing the technology of the chalumeau by first adding two keys and then gradually changing the size of the tone holes to improve intonation. Denner then relocated and added keys and a bell, increasing the length of the instrument. The result was a clarinet with an extended range to include the higher (clarion) register.

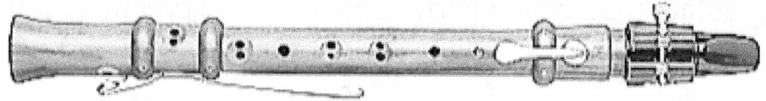

Early Clarinet

In the Middle Ages, the word clarion was applied to the trumpet. Because notes played on the clarinet in the upper register paralleled the intensity of those of a trumpet, the term was applied to that clarinet register. Combined with the chalumeau or lower register and eventually extending the range up to the altissimo, higher register, by 1800, the clarinet became the single reed instrument of choice, relegating the chalumeau instrument to a lesser status.

From then on, a series of artist/instrument makers modified the instrument over 300 years to the point where it is now the contemporary clarinet. During that period, Ivan Muller, Hyacinthe Klosé, Auguste Buffet, Theobald Boehm, Heinrich Joseph Baermann, Eugène Albert, and Adolphe Sax each contributed modifications that would result in the contemporary clarinet with a key system consisting of 17 to 22 keys and 4 to 6 rings.

Ivan Müller (1786–1854) invented the air-tight pad, making possible the addition of enough keys to facilitate playing chromatics on the clarinet. Müller pads replaced the flat brass keys with leather pads that did not cover the tone holes. Müller also invented the metal ligature, which replaced the string or wire used up to that point to secure the reed to the mouthpiece. An interesting note is that, to date, some clarinetists still prefer the use of string in place of a ligature.

In addition to inventing the air-tight pad and the ligature, Müller redesigned the clarinet to contain thirteen keys to service redesigned tone holes. The result was a greater facility for the player and improved intonation. Müller's system had no ring keys.

Müller System Clarinet

Eugene Albert (1816–1890) was a Belgian clarinet maker who developed a key system based on the Müller 13 key system but with the addition of two ring keys. Adolphe Sax, a clarinet maker and saxophone inventor, was Albert's tutor. Sax was responsible for adding the two ring keys to Albert's key system. After that, Albert added two rings, resulting in the "Albert System" with thirteen keys and four ring keys. This arrangement enhanced the intonation of the clarinet and once again made fingering and cross-fingering easier.

Albert's clarinets were very well received because of their excellent craftsmanship and intonation; however, there was one limitation. The instruments were made to pitch A=452 vibrations per second, meaning that the general intonation was higher than the standard A=440. Albert's son, also a clarinet maker, seeing his father's instruments going out of favor, built a clarinet to tune to A=440, extending the popularity of the Albert System clarinets into the twentieth century.

Albert System Clarinet

Hyacinthe Klosé (1808–1880), August Buffet (1789–1864), and the Boehm System—The Boehm key system, originally invented by Theobold Boehm for the flute, served as a model for Hyacinthe Klosé and August Buffet to create a key system for the clarinet. Over about four years, starting in 1839, they modified ring keys and side keys, enabling clarinetists to play chromatics and difficult passages with comparative ease and a much-improved intonation. Theobold Boehm had no part in this transition except to have been the inspiration for what is called the Boehm clarinet key system. In the last quarter of the nineteenth century, Buffet introduced the full Boehm system, which was accepted worldwide and replaced the Albert System.

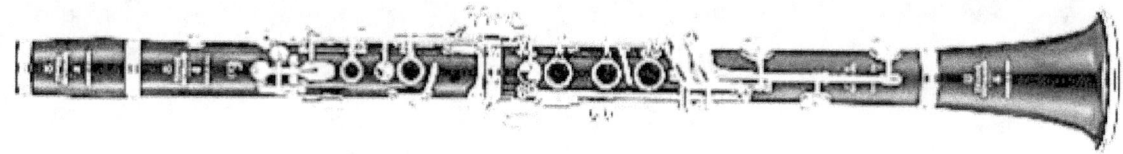

Boehm System Clarinet

Oskar Öhler (1858–1936) As clarinet technology developed to a point where a player could perform at a high level technically, a need grew to improve intonation and tone quality further. Öhler achieved this by repositioning the tone holes, modifying the fingering, and adding keys up to twenty-eight. He also reduced the diameter of the bore, extended its length, and decreased the diameter of the mouthpiece bore. Öhler's concepts for tone improvement were carried on by his students and eventually into the late twentieth century by the Wurlitzer Manufacturing Company, whose clarinets are most popular in Germany.

Öhler System Clarinet

The Saxophone

The saxophone can be considered the first woodwind instrument invented instead of being an offshoot of some instrument from the past.

Adolph Sax (1814–1894) born in Belgium, was a flutist, clarinetist, and instrument maker who received recognition for improving the timbre and key system and extending the lower range of the bass clarinet. He was also noted for making the ophicleide, a brass instrument played with a cup mouthpiece with tone holes fitted with as many as twelve woodwind-like padded keys.

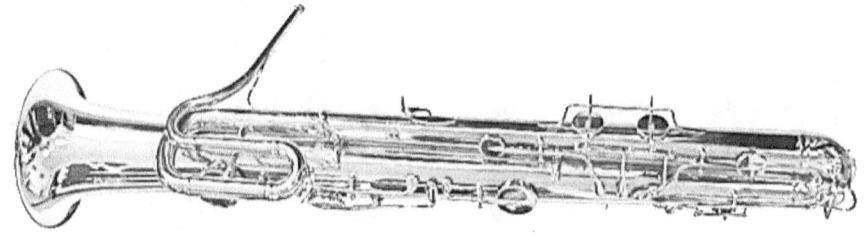

Ophicleide

With this background, we might guess that the stage was set in Sax's mind for a single reed woodwind instrument that would produce the sound characteristics of a brass instrument. Sax also intended to design an instrument to overblow at the octave rather than the twelfth, as does the clarinet to simplify the fingering. And so appeared the saxophone.

Sax designed and built a series of 14 saxophones spanning the tonal range from sopranino to contrabass. In 1846, he was granted a patent on these instruments, making him among the first instrument makers to design, build, and produce a woodwind instrument rather than evolving from a series of previous such instruments.

After the patent expired, several other makers improved the saxophone, enhanced the key system to facilitate playing legato passages and chromatics, changed the bell, and extended the instrument's range to F6. Modifying the key work replaced two octave keys that operated the two octave vents with one key to control both vents. The saxophone now holds an important position in all categories of instrumental music.

Below is a picture of the complete line of saxophones produced by the Selmer Musical Instrument Manufacturing Company. From left to right, they are the Eb Sopranino, Bb Soprano, Eb Alto, Bb Tenor, Eb Baritone, Bb Bass, and Eb Contrabass saxophones.

Saxophone Family Instruments

Saxophone Mouthpiece History

Progress in the study of the technology of musical instruments shows that an instrument's source of sound, namely the mouthpiece/reed, is primarily responsible for the quality of that sound. The mouthpiece is the major contributing factor to the quality of the tone produced. The saxophone's mouthpiece has proven to be an extreme example of this position. Saxophonists should select it carefully and consider their aptitude, physical characteristics, embouchure, and playing experience.

Many changes have taken place in the design of the saxophone's mouthpiece since the original was made in 1840. It has been lengthened, shortened, enlarged, made smaller, cored out, tapered, colored, and re-shaped using every sort of material conceivable. Each of these changes has contributed to the many opinions of the sound of the saxophone since each change in mouthpiece design resulted in a change in tone quality or timbre.

The sound generator (mouthpiece reed combination) is almost entirely responsible for the quality and timbre of the saxophone. The early alto saxophone mouthpiece had a tube-shaped bore with no taper. The throat was round, and the tone chamber had a bulbous portion preceding the window. The wall surfaces were concave, giving it a tone that was mellow and lacked the edge often associated with the saxophone.

The 1930s saw the era of the large dance band, which demanded a sound that would be better matched with brass instruments. At that time, the woodwind and brass instruments were distributed equally in these bands. It became necessary to strengthen the sound of the reeds to match that of the brasses.

Since sophisticated devices for sound evaluation were not yet available, those involved in research and development needed to rely on instinct to find remedies. They experimented with materials of various densities and expansion measurements and redesigned the structure of the mouthpiece interior. This experimentation produced many unsatisfactory mouthpieces that led to the decline of the reputation of the saxophone as a serious instrument.

During that time, one mouthpiece was developed, which modified the original and helped the saxophone regain some of its original popularity. The new model mouthpiece produced a richer tone, emphasizing the upper notes. Following that, the industry developed another design modeled on the shape of the clarinet mouthpiece. This mouthpiece produced an extraordinarily powerful and penetrating sound, and it gained favor from dance band music performers who competed with their brass-playing counterparts. Simultaneously, classical musicians stopped using the saxophone due to the instrument's increasing incompatibility with symphonic sounds.

Further experimentation with more advanced technological sound-evaluating devices led to smaller chambers, which proved unsatisfactory, and then to the double-tone chamber, which had a tapered cylindrical bore and a smaller tone chamber and throat. This mouthpiece produced a very aggressive sound, enabling a player to blast out the notes but creating a greater likelihood that the less experienced player might lose control of tone quality and intonation. A mouthpiece that seemed to strike a suitable balance, including most of the above features, produced a tone acceptable to most "classical" musicians. Having a round chamber, it produced a smooth, mellow tone yet with a bright edge.

Double Reed Instruments
The Oboe

The Shawm—Dating back to the twelfth century, the Shawm was a double reed, conical bore instrument with eight tone holes, seven on the front and one on the back. The reed on some ancient shawms was surrounded by a windcap called a pirouette. With this device in place, the player's lips had no direct contact with the reed, making it possible to play the instrument while on horseback or marching.

As stated above, the disadvantage of this arrangement was the player's lack of control of intonation, expression, and nuanced volume normally afforded by direct contact with the reed. The resulting sound was piercing and very rich in overtones. Its strident tone was intended to compete with and accompany trumpets and percussion instruments.

As the Shawm evolved, the tone quality was somewhat modified by a change in its architecture. The range was increased by an octave, and the bore and tone holes were reduced in size. Various-sized shawms were made to cover the range from soprano to bass, the latter being less than successful due to its inconvenient size. The Shawm enjoyed popularity up to the middle of the seventeenth century when the oboe began to make its presence known.

The Oboe—The oboe is a derivative of the Shawm but with a more advanced key system that permits the player to perform with reasonable ease. Removing the windcap gives the player direct contact with the double reed, improving intonation, timbre, and volume control. The result is an instrument compatible with a modern orchestra instead of the Shawm, which produces a more "independent" sound.

Shawm and Oboe

The oboe body was divided into three sections for convenient transportation and to facilitate repairs to the body. Damage to one section of a three-piece body is easier to deal with than damage to a one-piece body. A three-piece body can easily have a damaged section replaced without replacing the entire body.

In determining who invented the oboe, we can only guess based on word-of-mouth evidence from individuals in Europe's music world of the seventeenth-century era. Some historians credit Jean Hotteterre and Michel Danican Philidor as the inventors, separately or together.

The instrument known as the hautbois was a modification of the Shawm. The windcap was replaced by a double reed, and gradually, a key system evolved to accommodate the needs of the music. Four stages of development followed this. These were labeled Baroque, classical, Viennese, and conservatory models.

The original Baroque oboe was a simple instrument with three keys ranging from C4 to D6. To move to a higher register, the player had to increase the intensity of the air stream.

Baroque Oboe

During the classical period in music, a more advanced oboe was developed to satisfy the growing needs of the music performance community. The instrument had additional keys, a decreased bore diameter to ease playing in the upper register, and a vent key (not quite an octave key as we know it), which easily shifted up an octave. It was later in evolution that a true octave key was devised. The classical oboe range increased to F6.

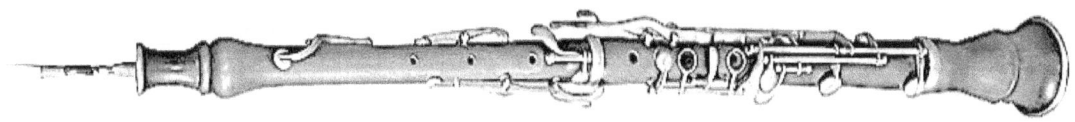

Classical Oboe

The Viennese oboe began appearing in the last quarter of the nineteenth century. This is a hybrid of oboes from the Austrian/German system with a larger bore and a more complex key system. The upper register was also stronger in timbre and projection due to increased upper partials. The larger bore, combined with wider and shorter reeds, produces a strong, double-reed sound with ease of playing. Note the differently shaped bell. The Viennese oboe might be considered the bridge from the antique to today's instrument. This instrument is still in use today.

Viennese Oboe

The Conservatory oboe was also developed at about the same time as the Viennese oboe and had a key system modeled after the Boehm oboe system. This system was not very popular but did act as the next step in developing the instrument to reach the point of the modern full Conservatory system now in use. The full conservatory system has forty-five keys, some with rings and others with plateau keys. These oboes have a range from Bb3 to A6.

Conservatory Oboe

The modern oboe is the one now in use. It is the product of all that preceded it, with an excellent but complex key system and bore dimensions that produce the oboe sound we all recognize. This general design is now made in many different models to satisfy the entire range of notes used in music today.

Modern Oboe

The Bassoon

The Bassoon—The Shawm, dulcian, and rankett are considered the forerunners of the bassoon. These instruments were popular for about two hundred years from the mid-sixteenth century. Like the bassoon, they used a double reed connected to a bocal. As the double reed shawm (described above) evolved into larger sizes, producing lower pitches, we could consider it the beginning of what would eventually become the bassoon.

The dulcian was a step closer to our current bassoon. Its bore was cone-shaped and long enough to be folded upon itself. However, unlike the bassoon, the dulcian was carved from one piece of maple.

The tone holes had to be drilled at an angle so that on the inside of the bore, they were placed according to the sound requirements, while on the outside of the instrument, they would fit a normal finger span of the player.

During the Dulcian period of popularity, eight different-sized versions were developed to complete the soprano to bass range. The instrument had eight tone holes and two keys. The dulcian continued to be popular as the bassoon began to make its appearance.

Dulcian

The rankett was also an instrument from the sixteenth century that may have added to the development of the bassoon in that the rankett was a double-reed instrument with a range as low as G2.

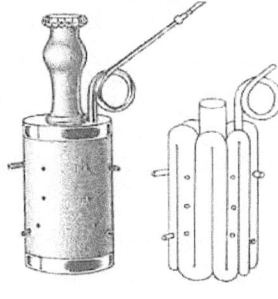

Rankett

(Compliments of Wikipedia)

The unique difference was that rather than having a straight bore found in other woodwind instruments, the rankett was about five inches long but achieved the low range through a cylindrical bore within the body with nine tone holes spaced to accommodate the spread of a player's hand.

Other modifications in the tone holes and bore were made by John Christian Denner. Denner advanced the technology of the chalumeau to the point where he made the first extended-range baroque bassoon. He developed the rankett to the point where it was, in effect, a small bassoon.

Jacques Martin Hotteterre (1673–1763), as mentioned above, Jacques devised the oboe with a three-piece design with a separate head joint, body, and foot joint structure. In addition to being a prominent flutist, composer, and Renaissance man in the music world of his time, he is credited with being one of several individuals responsible for developing the bassoon.

As a member of a large family of instrument makers, we might guess that Hotteterre was able to use his musical ability, experience, and creativity in conjunction with the skills of his instrument-maker family members to develop and build an early bassoon. Hotteterre is credited with increasing the bell's size, extending the bassoon's range, and designing the instrument in four sections so the bore could be more accurately machined.

Carl Almenraeder (1786–1846) is credited with designing a bassoon with 17 keys that could play a four-octave range chromatically. Almenraeder joined J.A. Heckel (1812–1877) in producing what would become the German Heckel system bassoon. Heckel went on to expand the bassoon range and create a contrabassoon. Both of these were prototypes for the bassoons used today.

The advancement of technology in musical instrument manufacturing and an increased understanding of the principles of acoustics enabled instrument makers to provide for the increased demands of the performing community. And so evolved the Heckle or German system and the Buffet or French system bassoons. These are two distinctly differently designed instruments that, to date, serve two differing viewpoints on what a bassoon should be.

The Heckel (German) system features a more complicated key system with up to 27 keys joined with a wider bore, producing a fuller sound. Heckel system bassoons currently enjoy popularity throughout most of the world, while the Buffet model has greater popularity in France, Spain, and Canada.

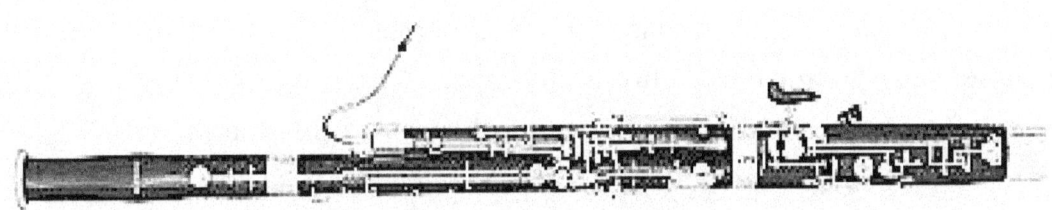

Heckel System Bassoon

The Buffet (French) design has a simple 22-key system joined with a narrow bore. The results are less complicated fingering requirements and more lyrical mellow tone quality.

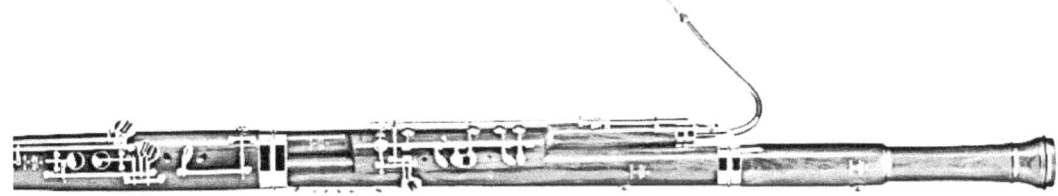

Buffet System Bassoon

Summary—The early history of woodwind instruments is, at best, vague and lacking in definitive structure. As far as we know, they began with the simple act of blowing air into some reed-like plant. Yet, they became more complex mechanically and acoustically than all the other instruments.

Because there is a shortage of documentation on the early phase of woodwind instrument history, it is necessary to guess their development. From Medieval times to the present, organologists (musical instrument scientists) have access to an almost overwhelming amount of documented history on how woodwind instruments began to be crafted and developed to the point at which we now enjoy their use.

The instruments of the woodwind family provide the music community with a listening pleasure that spans most of the notes with any emotion, from expressive lyricism to dynamic brilliance. These instruments can stand on their own as solo instruments, be part of a woodwind ensemble, or contribute to the sounds of any other combination of musical instruments. In a symphony orchestra, they are the core of the auditory transition between the string and brass sections.

From the primitive individuals who made the first sounds with a bamboo reed to the inventors, musicians, technicians, and visionaries who brought us up to the point where society is now fortunate enough to enjoy a listening experience that has become a precious possession of our music world, a profound thank you!

Chapter 8

What Items (Accessories) Will I Need to Help Me Play My Bassoon?

To function properly, musical instruments require accessories. Three categories of accessories available to enhance the playing experience are those that are necessary, those that make playing easier and maintain an instrument, and those that are luxuries.

The following accessories are needed to successfully play and maintain any of the instruments in the bassoon family. Because of the many brands of each product on the market, I will discuss this topic in general terms.

Lubricants—Bassoons have many moving parts which require regular lubrication. Searching for "bassoon lubricants" in Google Images will illustrate the variety of available products. The following is a description of different types of lubricants and their use.

Using Oil—The figure below shows key oil in a needle-type dispenser for easy distribution. The bore oil bottle is typical of those used for that product. The oils you use for each process will have to be your decision. Use the following information to start your search on the subject. Note the oils that are packaged with a needle applicator. Those are very convenient.

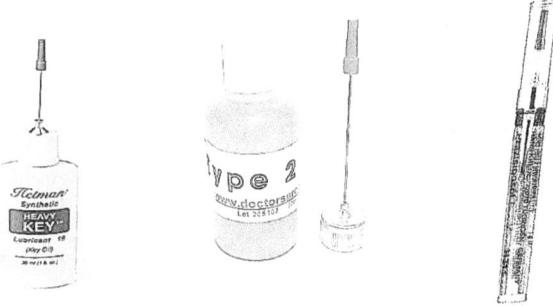

Key Oil Dispensers

Selecting Key Oil—To decide how long an oil will work successfully before evaporating, rub a drop of oil between your thumb and index finger and judge how long the oil's oiling sensation lasts. Compare several oils against one another. Petroleum-based oils will probably last a shorter time than synthetic oils. The choice of oil is a very individual one.

Light oil tends to evaporate more quickly than thicker oils. Light oil tends to travel down the post to the instrument's body. This is messy if the body is plastic, destructive if the body is wood, will collect dust and lint, and can loosen the adhesive on any cork the oil may contact.

A review of what you learned in chapter 5. To test the viscosity (thickness) of oil, start by shaking the bottle to see how the contents move. The slower the oil moves, the thicker it is.

To compare the thickness of several oils, place a drop of each, side by side, on one end of a smooth, flat surface. Then, raise that end of the surface and note the rate of speed at which the oils travel downward. Thicker oils will move more slowly. With several choices, try each on one key of your bassoon using a different key for each trial. Do not combine different oils during the trial.

Cork Grease—Chapter 5 teaches you how to use cork grease. There are numerous brands available, each claiming its virtues above the others. Each manufacturer has its formula based on assorted oils.

Different Packaging of Cork Grease

Cleaning Brushes—Bassoon bocal and key cleaning brushes are available in a variety of shapes and sizes suited for every possible use. Below are a bocal brush, key duster, and two general-purpose brushes.

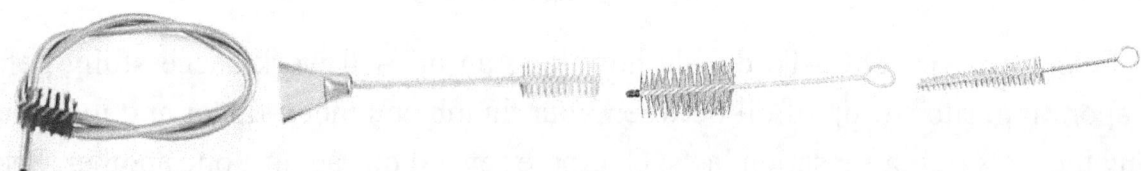

Cleaning Brushes

Tuning Forks—Invented in 1711 by John Shore, the tuning fork is the most basic device designed to determine pitch accurately. The device consists of a U-shaped metal form with a handle at the base of the U. Holding the tuning fork by the handle when the tines (prongs) are struck on a hard surface, they are set into a vibrating pattern, which produces a tone.

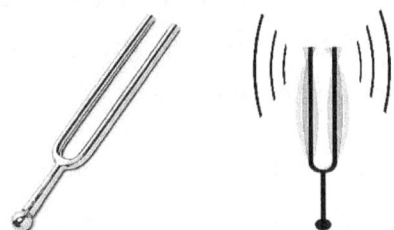

Tuning Fork and One with Vibrating Tines

Pitch Pipes—A chromatic pitch pipe is round and contains a marked opening for every pitch in the chromatic scale. The notes start at C and progress chromatically up an octave to the next C in the scale. You can choose any note, slide the white marker to that note's position on the pitch pipe, blow into that hole, and hear the pitch selected.

Chromatic Pitch Pipe

Electronic Tuners—Below are pictured two kinds of electronic tuners. One type offers a three-in-one calibrator, tuner, and metronome, and the other is a clip-on showing a big LED display of the pitches you are tuning. When you play a note, the screen will show if the sound is sharp, flat, or spot-on. You can adjust the bassoon or your embouchure until the correct pitch is reached.

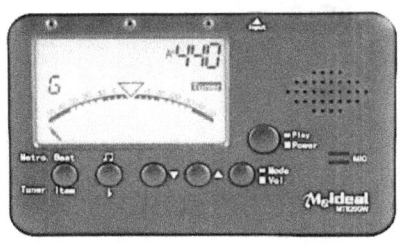 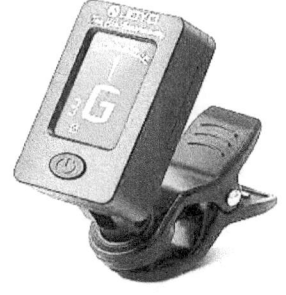

Electronic Tuners

Apps or Applications—Aids to tuning appear on websites, iPads, cell phones, and the Internet. Use them wisely, but try to avoid being distracted by the charm of technology.

Summary of Tuners—In this writing, Amazon.com shows five pages, each with about fifteen different tuners for a total of seventy-five tuners of all kinds now on the market. The choices start with a simple, inexpensive device with a chromatic scale into which you can blow to produce the desired pitch to match.

The advantage of using this product is that it requires you to listen to and think of pitch instead of relying on visual aids to tune. Music is a hearing art, so every act that will help train your ear to hear and your mind to think of sound is another step toward success.

Electric Pickups—Amplified bassoons share the same basic sound equipment as electric guitars. These include pickups, pre-amplifiers, amplifiers, equalizers, and speakers.

Acoustic Electric Bassoons—An amplified bassoon is a traditional instrument to which a pickup is added. Two kinds of pickups in general use are the magnetic pickup, which is built into parts of the instrument's body, and a microphone in various locations depending on the instrument. Below is a magnetic pickup built into a bassoon bocal.

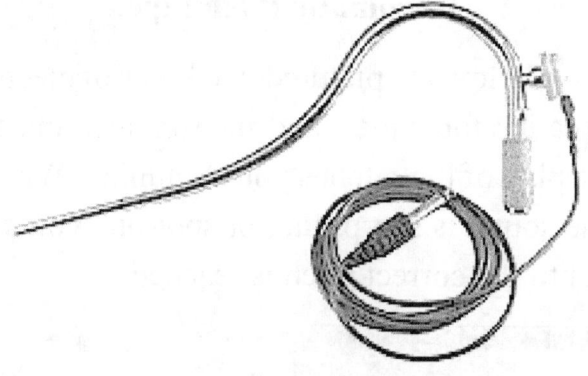

Magnetic Pickup

The pickups are connected with a cable to an amplifying system. With the proper equipment, pickups can also be wireless.

The condenser microphone is most popular because of its low cost and true sound. This microphone converts sound waves into electrical energy and sends it to an amplifier and a speaker. A condenser microphone can easily be clipped onto almost any instrument, and you have an amplified (electric) instrument.

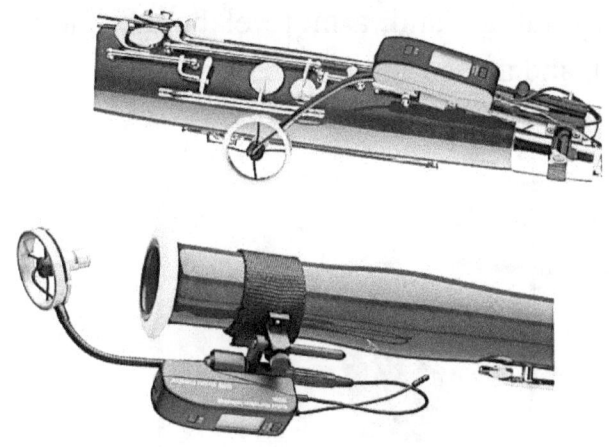

Clip On Microphones

The term used to define this type of microphone is cardioid, which can pick up sound from an area of 180 degrees from the front with fading reception beyond that radius.

The downside to this microphone is that while it will pick up the bassoon's sound, it will also pick up surrounding sounds caused by handling the instrument, such as bumps, knocks, and sometimes even the action of the keys in motion. There is also a danger of feedback when using this type of microphone.

Music Stands—Correct posture and playing position are essential to successful performance on any instrument. A music stand is a very important aid in keeping that posture. Music stands are sold in three basic designs. Some stands fold, others are rigid or non-folding, and there are tabletop versions.

The folding or sheet music stand is very useful for a beginning student. It is lightweight, totally portable, and very inexpensive. Folding stands can also be purchased with a carrying case for more convenient portability. These stands can easily be knocked over, and the lightweight parts can be bent out of shape.

The rigid design stand, sometimes called a concert, stage, or orchestra music stand, is not convenient to carry, usually quite heavy, and is intended to be used in one place. This model stand is more expensive than the folding stand but is very stable, able to hold a good amount of music, and is practically indestructible.

Below is a simple folding stand, a more elaborate one with a carrying case, a ridged orchestra stand, and a decorative model.

Music Stands

A tabletop stand is small, very portable, does not have legs, and is lightweight and inexpensive. It can be placed on any stable surface for complete flexibility. The problem is that if it is on a tabletop, the music could be too low for you to see while standing and keeping a proper playing position. A folding, decorative, and concert tabletop stand is pictured below.

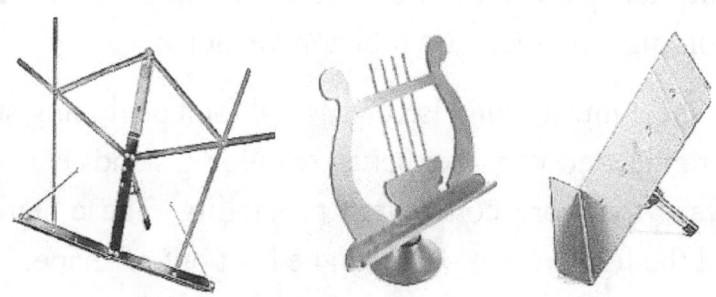

Tabletop Stands

Swabs—Swabs are essential for the care of your bassoon. The figures below show a pull-through bocal swab, a bocal brush, a wing joint, and a boot joint swab. See chapter 5 for information on using swabs.

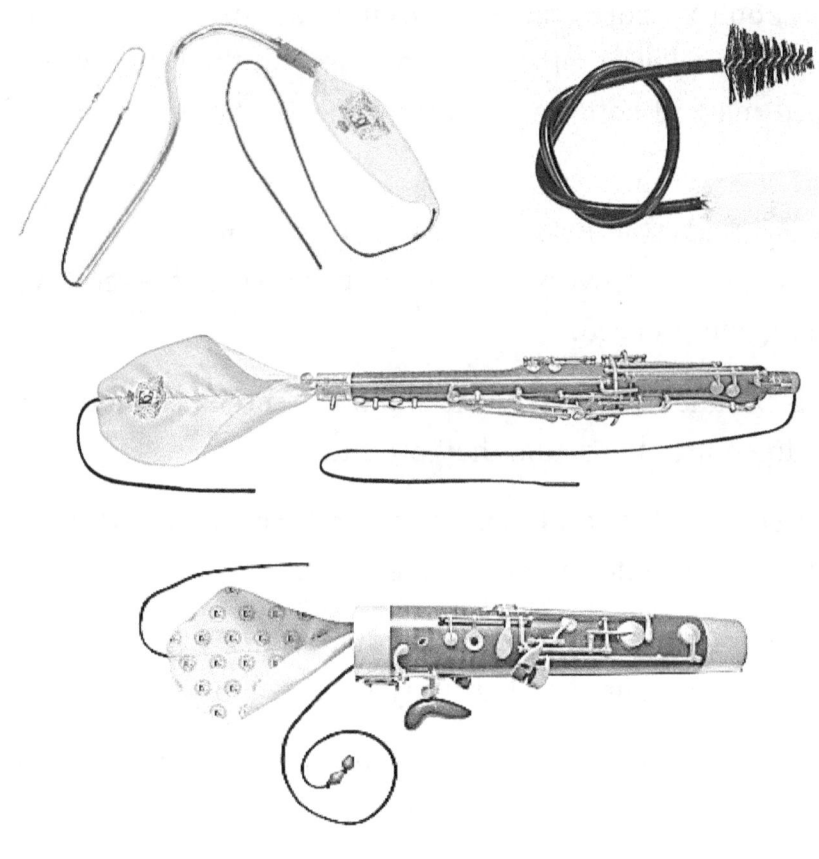

Swabs

Neck Straps—A neck strap helps you easily hold your bassoon during long playing sessions. The figure below shows three different kinds of bassoon straps. There are more.

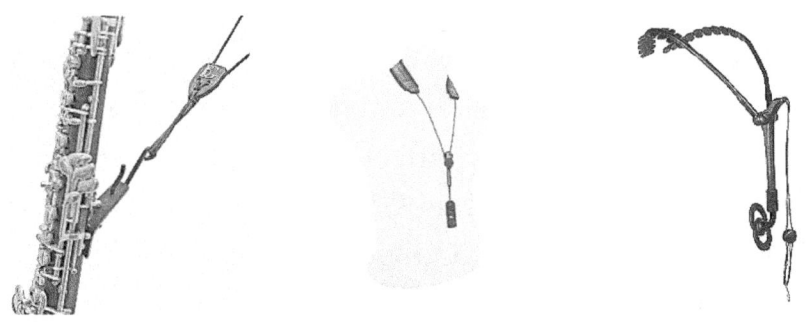

Bassoon Neck Straps

Bassoon Reeds—Double reeds are the source of sound for bassoons. Better reeds produce better sounds, so learning as much as possible about reeds is valuable.

The two major types of reeds now on the market are those made of cane called Arundo Donax, a distant relative of bamboo, and those made of various synthetic materials. Bassoon reeds are graded in strength as soft, medium-soft, medium, medium-hard, and hard. These ratings do not apply in the same way to different reed makers. A reed marked soft from one maker may be less than soft from another maker.

When buying reeds, the first step is to choose from famous makers. Don't rely on the maker's claims. Ask everyone you know who uses the reeds you are interested in, their opinion, and proceed.

Softer reeds produce a brighter tone and do so more easily, but they may be a bit more difficult to control the sound they produce.

A harder reed will give a bolder sound and can have difficulty playing in the lower register, but it is better in the high register.

Cane reeds should be some shade of medium to dark yellow. This shows that the wood has been properly cured and is ready for use. Do not buy a green reed.

Because the upper part of a reed is translucent, you can hold it up to a light and see its inner structure. It is best if the vertical fibers are evenly spaced, parallel, and have a consistent color.

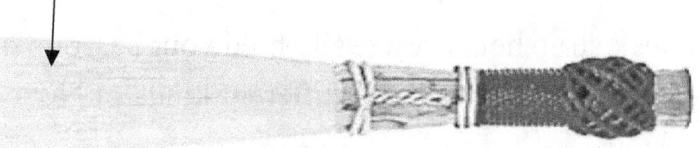

Bassoon reeds come in three different "scrapes." The term "scrape" refers to the final shaping of a reed where a certain amount of wood is scraped off the reed's surface. How the reed is scraped will affect the sound it produces. Three different styles of possible scrapes are American, German, and French. As you read on, remember that bassoon reeds are very individual, so it is not likely to find any two reeds exactly the same.

American Scrape Reeds—Producing a tone and articulating from note to note on an American scrape reed is relatively easy, requiring average airflow effort. Intonation is also easy to maintain while using a comfortable embouchure. These reeds will usually produce an acceptable bassoon tone quality and intonation.

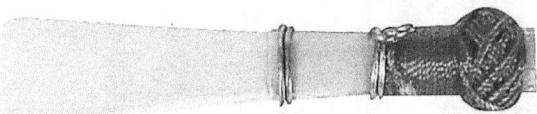

German Scrape Reeds—Producing a tone and articulating from note to note is more challenging than the American scrape reed. Performing on this reed requires a stronger embouchure with a more forceful airflow output. Maintaining correct intonation and articulation also requires greater effort. A strong embouchure pressure is also needed to produce a resonant tone quality.

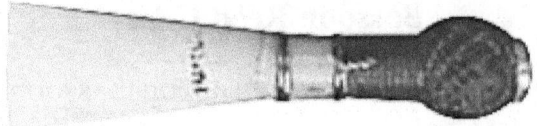

French Scrape Reeds—Producing a tone and articulating notes is generally the easiest of the three style reeds, except for notes in the lower register. In that range, greater embouchure and airflow force are needed. With this cut reed, keeping a correct pitch is not difficult, except for notes in the upper register. There is a greater chance of intonation issues because of the instability of pitch control. Timbre production with this type of reed can be easily altered with embouchure to suit the playing needs.

Plastic Reeds—Plastic reeds copy the natural fibers of a cane reed with artificial fibers made of synthetic polymers. These reeds look, feel, and, in the opinion of many, sound like traditional cane reeds. Plastic reeds are durable, consistent in their structure, reliable in their sound production, and have a long lifespan. The figure below shows a plastic bassoon reed.

Reed Cases—Reed cases pay for themselves by preventing reeds from being damaged in transit or storage. The figure below shows a three-reed case, one for many reeds and one with a humidifier to prevent reeds from drying out.

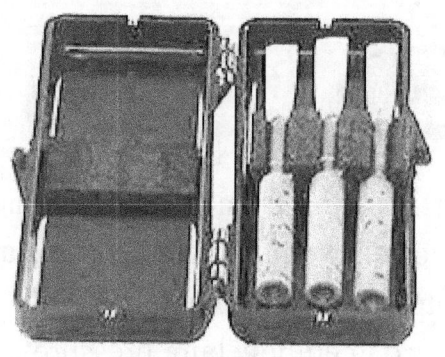 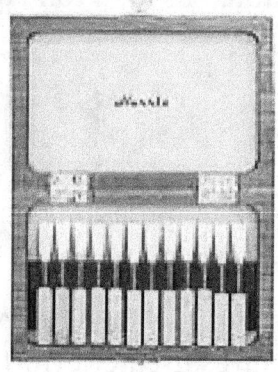 

Bassoon Reed Cases

Bassoon Screwdrivers—The screws used on bassoon key mechanisms have very small, slotted heads. Use the correct size screwdriver to turn or remove one of these screws. A screwdriver with a head that is a bit too small but does fit in the screw slot may allow the screwdriver to slip out of the screw slot and possibly strip the screw head.

The figure below shows two sets of screwdrivers suited to working with most bassoon key systems. Remember, do not force a screw that does not respond immediately. Bring the instrument to a professional.

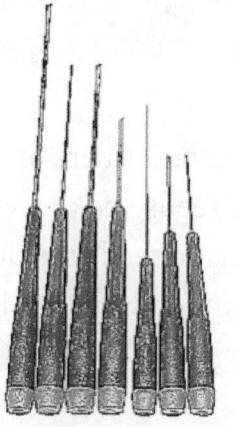 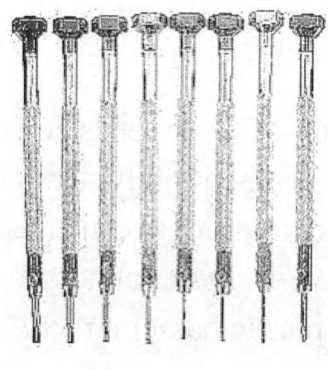

Bassoon Screwdrivers

Lyres—A lyre is a portable music stand. It is attached to an instrument and goes wherever the instrument goes. Lyres are used to hold the music for marching band instruments.

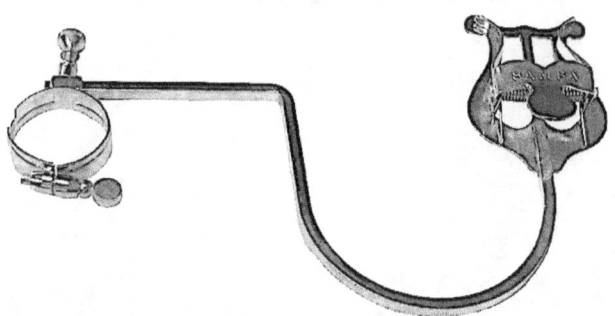

Bassoon Lyre

Instrument Stands—A stand is designed to safely hold every bassoon when not in use. Since there are so many different stands, it is best to search "bassoon stands" on Google Images and scroll down to see the wide variety available. Click on the picture of the one you like best, then click on the "visit page" for additional information on the product. When you find something interesting, your best move might be to order it online if the return policy is favorable. If you prefer to shop directly, print the page of the desired product and begin the search at your local music store. Below are pictures of a bassoon stand and a combination bassoon and contrabassoon stand.

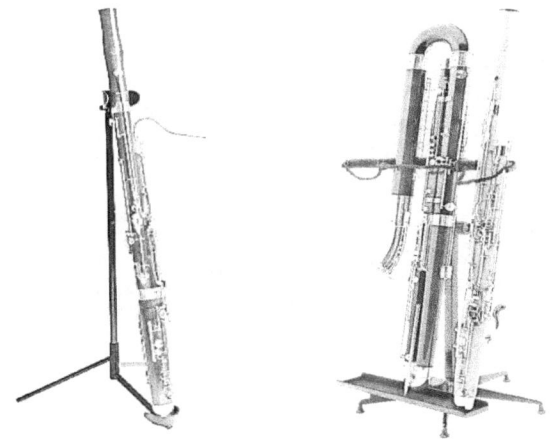

Bassoon Stands

Bassoon Cases—Cases are available in hard and soft models. Soft cases are often called "gig bags." If padded, they will provide sufficient protection for normal use. A hard case is best if the instrument is to travel or be transported by young players. Below are pictured three kinds of gig bags for bassoons.

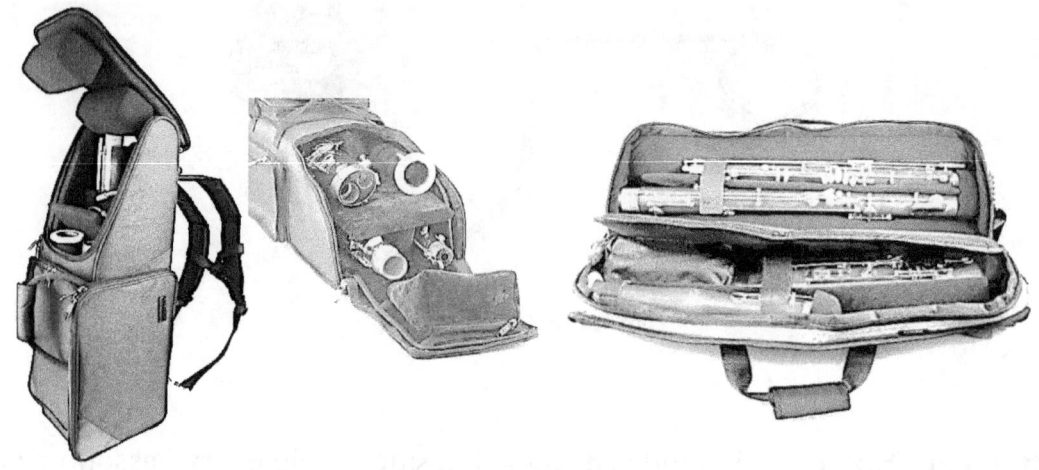

Soft Bassoon Cases

Hard cases are heavier than soft cases but offer greater protection for the instrument. Some hard cases are made of wood and are covered with various durable fabrics. The inner linings are shaped to fit the instrument, padded, and often lined with velour. A simpler and usually less expensive construction for a hard case is lightweight and durable molded plastic with an inner lining of soft padding with plush fabric. The figures below show two differently shaped bassoon hard cases. There are many more.

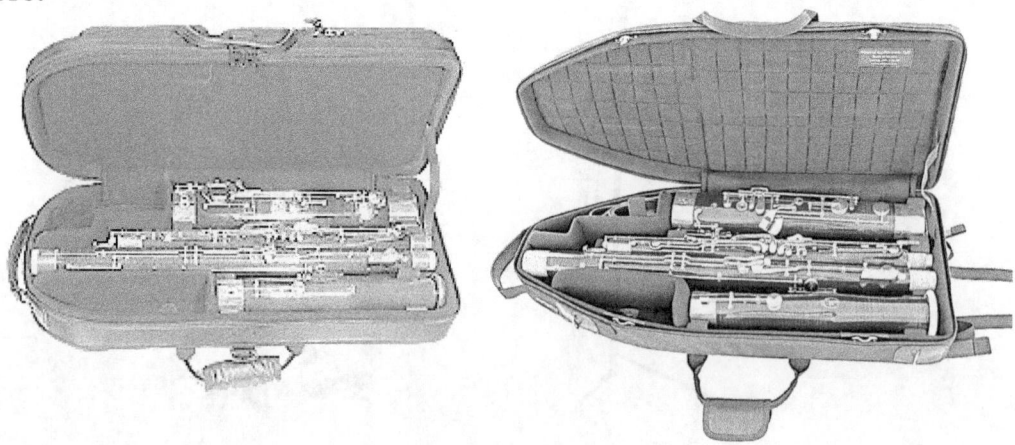

Bassoon Hard Cases

Summary—The introduction to this chapter states that musical instrument accessories fall into the categories of those that are necessary, those that make playing more enjoyable, and those that are luxuries. These three categories are not divided by strict rules. What may be one person's luxury could well be considered by another to be a necessity. As is usually the case in music, the decision is unique to the individual. The examples in this chapter sample what is available in each category. There are, in fact, hundreds of additional variations on the market.

NOTES

Appendix

Note: In this appendix, you will learn words used in the study of the science of sound. When these words appear, they will be followed by the more common term in parentheses.

Scientific Pitch Notation—The following explains a system used throughout music study called ***Scientific Pitch Notation***. This is a valuable tool that can serve you throughout your music career.

Scientific Pitch Notation helps you know exactly where a note is located on the staff without seeing the note in print. This system uses alphanumerics (a combination of letters and numerals) to tell you exactly where a note is in the entire range of notes. An example would be middle C, whose alphanumeric name is C4. The C one octave below middle C is C3. The C an octave above middle C is C5. The notes going up between these Cs keep the C's numeral until the next C is reached. Examples would be C4, D4, E4, F4, G4, A4, B4, C5, D5, etc. The figure below shows the alphanumeric symbol for all notes.

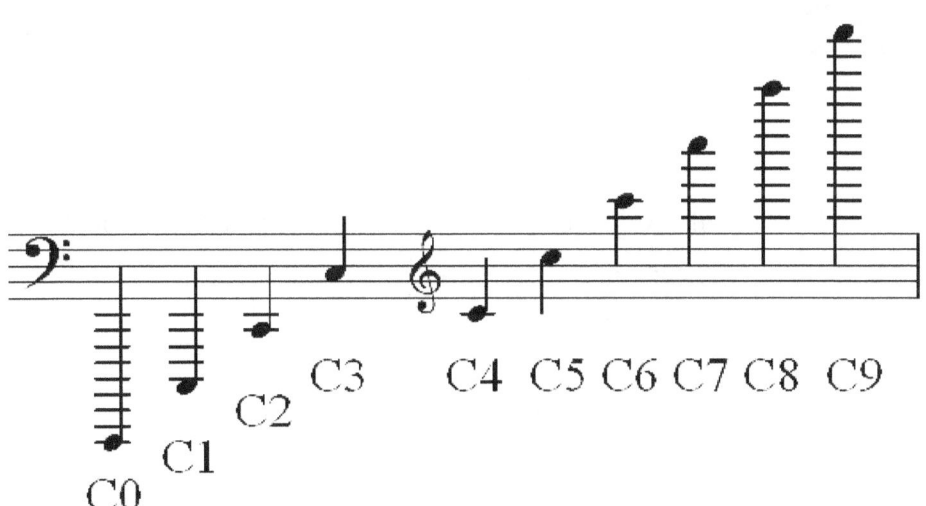

Sound—Sound occurs when something causes vibrations in the air. The vibrations travel by waves of air pushed against one another, acting as a train would when the last car is pushed, and each car in front of the last one moves. This is called a chain reaction.

Molecules (tiny bits) of air push against one another to make sound travel. The grouping of tight molecules pictured below is named compression. The more open pattern is called rarefaction.

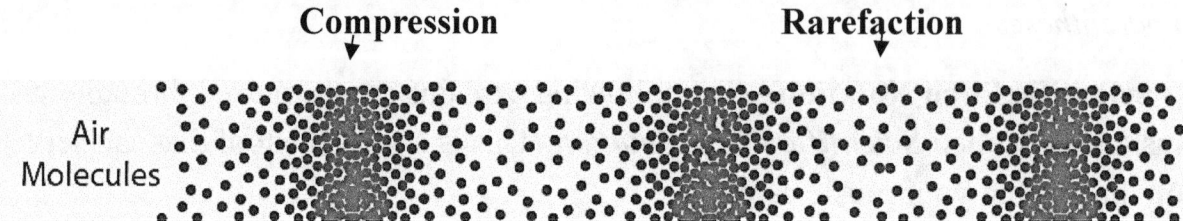

The combined action of compression and rarefaction results in a complete cycle of sound.

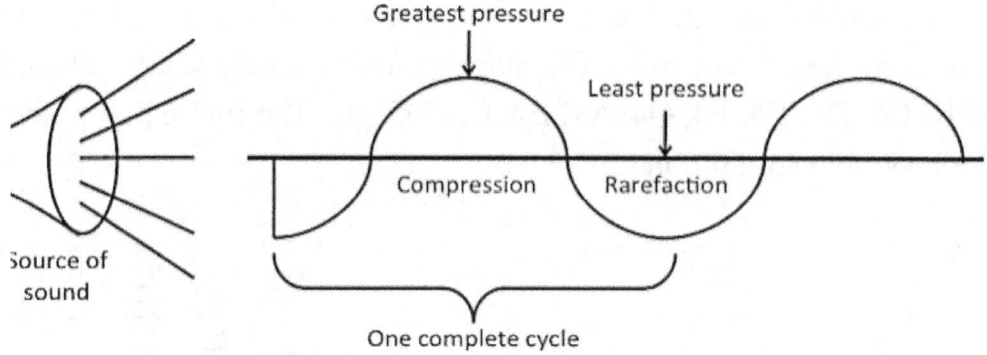

Vibration—If you look very closely at a guitar string that has been plucked, you will see that it moves very rapidly from side to side.

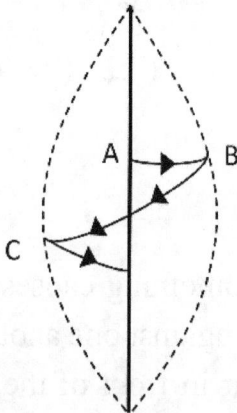

It moves from the center (A) to one side (B) and back across the center (A) to the other side (C). This entire voyage completes *one cycle*.

Cycles per Second (cps) or Hertz (Hz) (named after the physicist Heinrich Hertz) refers to the number of complete cycles per second, so 30 Hz means 30 cycles per second. Any tone results from the number of vibrations or cycles per second. "A" 440 is the tone produced by an instrument producing 440 vibrations or cycles per second. Below are some examples of notes with their cps.

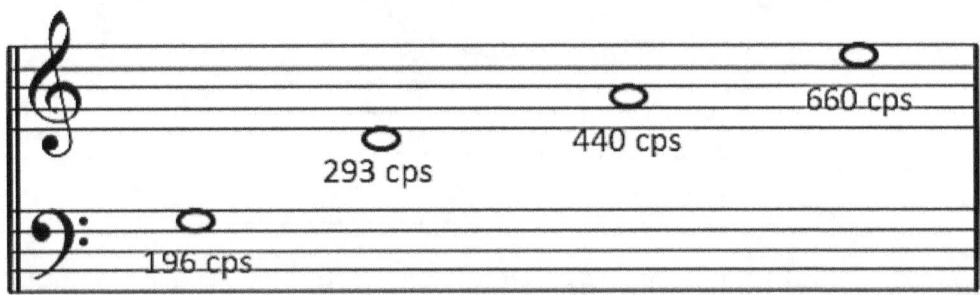

Cycles per Second

Sine Wave—When sound is created on a musical instrument, it produces a pattern of vibrations. These vibrations include a fundamental (basic) pitch and several other related pitches with less amplitude (volume). The fundamental pitch alone is a *pure tone* and can be pictured as a simple wave.

Pure Tone

Amplitude—Amplitude refers to the volume or loudness of a sound. Greater amplitude produces louder sounds. Less amplitude produces softer sounds.

Harmonics—When a pure tone is produced on a bassoon, it is joined by a series of related sounds or tones called harmonics. Other terms used for harmonics are overtones or upper partials. Any of these three terms can be used.

Harmonics (overtones or upper partials) are less important vibrations sounding with the fundamental (basic pitch) but with less amplitude (volume).

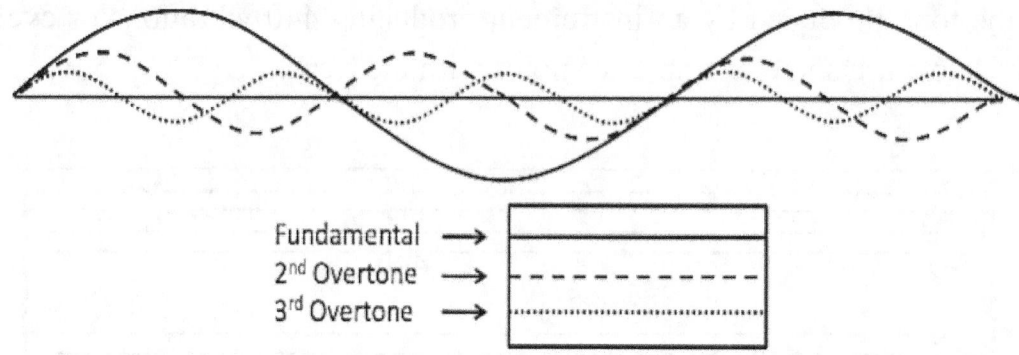

Harmonics cannot be heard as notes but are additions to the fundamental (basic pitch). Combining a basic pitch with harmonics creates the pitch's timbre (individual sound).

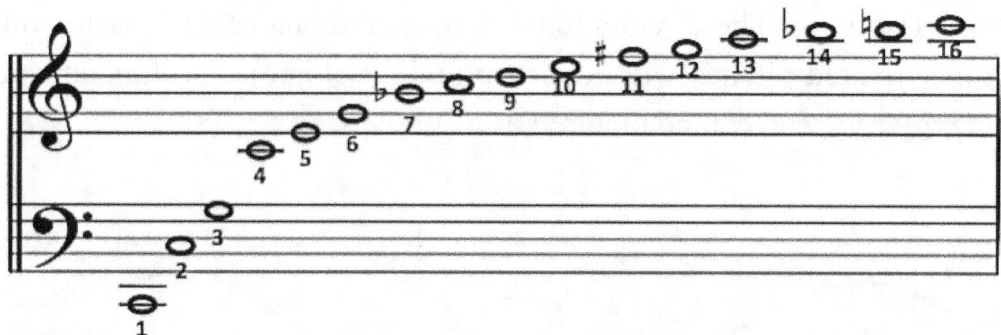

Harmonic Sequence

Timbre—Timbre is the product of adding tones to a fundamental pitch. These additional sounds, referred to as harmonics (overtones or upper partials), result from the built-in sound features of the instrument producing the sound. For the note C, these sounds follow the harmonic sequence pictured above and are present in most tones. The same interval pattern would occur for any note.

The difference in timbre results from the amplitude of the harmonics and how they relate in volume to the fundamental pitch. Stronger harmonics produce a timbre of greater intensity. Less amplitude of the harmonics will produce a less intense timbre. Tones played on the oboe have strong harmonics, producing a tone that can be identified as having an intense timbre. On the other hand, the flute has a comparatively weak set of harmonics and produces a more mellow tone.

Tone is a combination of pitch, volume, and timbre (the special quality of a pitch).

Pitch is the highness or lowness of a tone. The notes of an ascending scale (do, re, mi, fa, sol, la, ti, do) go up in pitch or are successively higher. The notes go down in pitch or are successively lower in a descending scale (do, ti, la, sol, fa, mi, re, do).

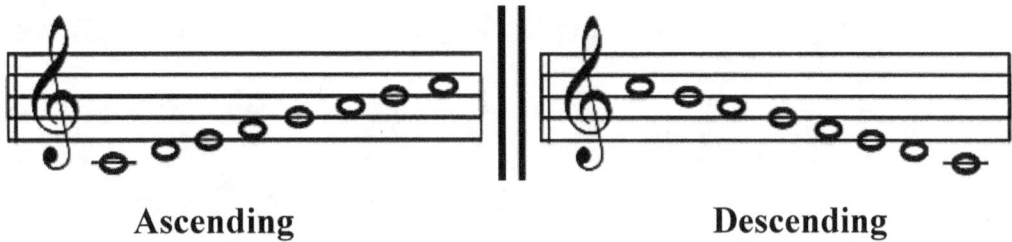

Ascending   **Descending**

Any series of notes can take one of only three possible directions in pitch. They can ascend (A), descend (B), or remain the same (C).

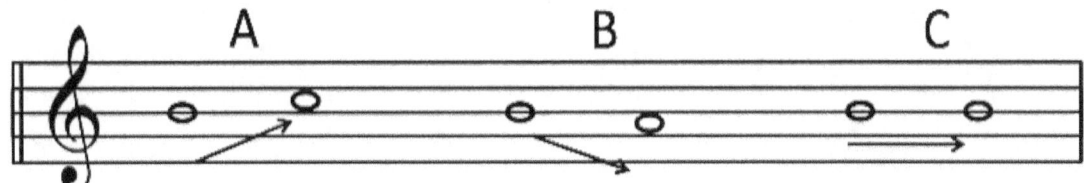

Summary—As you study your instrument, you are learning how to read music, use that information to work the mechanics of your bassoon to produce sounds, and then, using your artistic sense, turn those sounds into music. A terrific achievement. However, there is an underlying study that is not usually given much attention. That is the study of sound.

The chapter you just read gives you a very slight overview of some of the many topics in that subject. You learned words like scientific pitch notation, vibrations, compression, rarefaction, cycles per second, tone, amplitude, and harmonics. Those are just a few topics that are in the study of sound.

As you progress in your studies of the bassoon, include some of these sound topics, and you will be able to apply that knowledge to your music performance and be a better, more knowledgeable musician.

NOTES

Glossary of Woodwind Instrument Terms

Adjustment Screws—a screw that facilitates key adjustments to close tolerance.

Alphasax—a redesigned saxophone for smaller players.

Annealing—applying heat to brass to change its molecular structure.

Aulos—an ancient Greek flute-like instrument found in Greek iconography.

Baffle—the lower part of the reed side of a single reed mouthpiece.

Baroque—a decorative performance style or any art form practiced during the seventeenth and eighteenth centuries.

Bassoon—a double reed woodwind instrument with a range of about two octaves producing tones strong in upper partials.

Bell—the flared end of a bassoon from which the sound enters the atmosphere.

Bell Joint—the last section of a bassoon.

Billet—a section of wood in the first stages of woodwind construction.

Boot Joint (bass joint)—the second and lowest section of a bassoon body.

Bore—the inner tube of a musical instrument in which the vibrating column of air becomes a tone.

Clarineo Lyons C Clarinet—A lightweight modification of the Bb bassoon designed for young students.

Classical Music—Music composed during the eighteenth through the nineteenth century.

Closed Hole—a woodwind instrument key with a pad covering a tone hole.

Conservatory System—the key system on an oboe.

Contrabassoon—a lower-pitched version of a bassoon.

Cork Pads—pads made of cork used on woodwind instrument keys.

Crown—the first section of a flute head joint.

Crumhorn—a double reed woodwind windcap instrument from the Renaissance period.

Double Reed—a two-bladed reed used without a mouthpiece on instruments in the oboe and bassoon families.

Ebonite—a manmade hard rubber product used to make woodwind instrument bodies.

Facing—the upper segment of the reed side of a single reed mouthpiece.

Finger—(paddle) the section of a woodwind key where the player's finger is applied.

Fingering—the pattern used on the keys of a woodwind instrument to play a note.

Fish Skin Pads—fish skin used to cover the contact surface of some woodwind instrument pads.

Flat Shelf—the edge shelf section of a flute head joint embouchure hole.

Flat Spring—one of three types of springs used to return a key to its rest position.

Fulcrum—the pivot point on a woodwind instrument key.

Fundamental—the basic pitch upon which overtones are built.

Grenadilla—a close-grained, dark-colored, dense wood used to make woodwind instrument bodies.

Harmonics—pitches related to a fundamental pitch but sounding in lesser degrees of amplitude or volume.

Head Joint— the first section of a flute. A head joint has an embouchure hole into which the player blows air to produce a sound.

Intonation—the degree of accuracy with which a pitch is produced. A note can be in tune, sharp, or flat.

Key Pad Cup—the part of a woodwind key into which a pad is placed to cover a tone hole.

Key Springs—springs made of wire, blue steel, or other alloys installed to return a woodwind key to its original point of rest.

Key System—an arrangement of keys on a woodwind instrument.

Kinder Klari—a small E-flat clarinet modified to facilitate use by small hands.

Lay—(facing) the upper section of the reed side of a single reed mouthpiece.

Leather Pads—leather in place of fish skin used to surface the contact side of a woodwind instrument keypad.

Ligature—a band of metal or other material used to hold a reed on a single reed mouthpiece.

Lower Joint—the lower section of the body of a bassoon.

Mouthpiece—the first part of a woodwind instrument into which the player will blow to produce sound.

Neck—the uppermost section of a saxophone onto which the mouthpiece is connected.

Open Hole—a woodwind instrument key with a cup with a hole in its center.

Pad—a soft, fish skin or leather padded disc in woodwind instrument key pad cups that make contact with and seal tone holes.

Paddle—the part of a woodwind key that the player's finger contacts.

Pitch—the highness or lowness of a tone.

Plateau Keys—see closed hole.

Posts—knob-like elements holding the keys onto the body of a woodwind instrument.

Professional Level—the highest quality musical instrument.

Reed—a formed strip of cane used as a sound generator on woodwind instruments.

Resonator—a hard surfaced disc added to the center of a keypad to increase the resonance of a woodwind instrument.

Resonite—acrylonitrile butadiene styrene (ABS) is used to make bodies for inexpensive woodwind instruments.

Rib Construction—a strip of metal used to reinforce posts on flutes and saxophones.

Rosewood—a beautifully grained lighter, colored wood used to make bassoon bodies.

Saxonette—a clarinet-like instrument with a neck and upturned bell used as a transitional instrument between the clarinet and saxophone.

Saxophone—a single reed, brass-bodied woodwind instrument with padded keys.

Scientific Pitch Notation—an alphanumeric system combining letters and numbers to identify the location of a note on the staff.

Shawm—a double reed, wind-capped predecessor to the oboe and bassoon, popular in the Medieval and Renaissance periods.

Side Rails—the two narrow sides of a single reed mouthpiece bore.

Silicon Pads—a durable pad with a silicon surface used on woodwind instruments.

Single-Reed Mouthpiece—designed to use a single reed, typically for a clarinet or saxophone.

Sonic Welding—high-frequency sound waves used to install posts on plastic instrument bodies.

Sound Production—the process unique to each instrument used to generate sound.

Spatula—the fingered part of a woodwind instrument key.

Spring—strips of various metal alloys used to return a woodwind instrument key to its resting position.

Staple—the cork-covered tubular bottom of a double reed inserted into an instrument.

Step-Up (Intermediate)—the next step-up in quality and workmanship from a student-level musical instrument.

Student-Level—the least expensive entry-level musical instrument.

Tenon—the projection that joins each section of a woodwind instrument.

Throat—the inner section of a single reed mouthpiece between the chamber and the bore.

Tip Rail—the rounded top edge of the window of a single reed mouthpiece.

Tone Holes—holes in the body of a woodwind instrument used to change pitches.

Transposition—changing any combination of notes to a different key.

Triple Reed—a reed with three blades.

Tuning—the act of adjusting the pitch of an instrument.

Upper Joint—the upper section of the body of a woodwind instrument.

Windcap—a cylinder that encapsulates a double reed.

Window—the opening between the rails of a single reed mouthpiece.

Wing Joint—the first section of a bassoon's body after the bocal.

Zummara—a two-bodied nineteenth-century mid-eastern woodwind instrument.

NOTES

Dictionary of Bassoon Terms

For your convenience, this dictionary is a review of <u>bassoon-only terms</u> from the woodwind glossary above.

Bell—The flared end of a bassoon from which the sound enters the atmosphere.

Bell Joint—the last section of a bassoon.

Billet—a section of wood in the first stages of bassoon construction.

Boot Joint (bass Joint)—the second and lowest section of a bassoon body.

Bore—the inner tube of a musical instrument in which the vibrating column of air becomes a tone.

Bassoon—a category of double reed woodwind instruments.

Clarineo Lyons C Clarinet—A lightweight modification of a bassoon designed for young students.

Contrabassoon—a lower-pitched version of a bassoon.

Crumhorn—a double reed woodwind windcap instrument from the Renaissance period.

Double Reed—a two-bladed reed used without a mouthpiece on instruments in the oboe and bassoon families.

Ebonite—a manmade hard rubber product used to make bassoon bodies.

Finger—(paddle) the section of a woodwind key where the player's finger is applied.

Fingering—the pattern used on the keys of a bassoon to play a note.

Flat Spring—one of three types of springs used to return a key to its rest position.

Fulcrum—the pivot point on a bassoon key.

Fundamental—the basic pitch upon which overtones are built.

Grenadilla—a close-grained, dark-colored, dense wood used to make bassoon bodies.

Harmonics—pitches related to a fundamental pitch but sounding in lesser degrees of amplitude or volume.

Intonation—the degree of accuracy with which a pitch is produced. A note can be in tune, sharp, or flat.

Key Pad Cup—the part of a bassoon key into which a pad is placed to cover a tone hole.

Key Springs—springs made of wire, blue steel, or other alloys installed to return a bassoon key to its original point of rest.

Key System—an arrangement of keys on a bassoon.

Leather Pads—leather in place of fish skin used to surface the contact side of a bassoon keypad.

Pad—a soft, fish skin or leather padded disc in bassoon key pad cups that make contact with and seal tone holes.

Paddle—the part of a bassoon key that the player's finger contacts.

Pitch—the highness or lowness of a tone.

Posts—knob-like elements holding the keys onto the body of a bassoon.

Professional Level—the highest quality musical instrument.

Reed—formed cane strips used as a sound generator on bassoons.

Resonite—acrylonitrile butadiene styrene (ABS) is used to make bodies for inexpensive bassoons.

Rosewood—a beautifully grained lighter, colored wood used to make bassoon bodies.

Scientific Pitch Notation—an alphanumeric system combining letters and numbers to identify the location of a note on the staff.

Shawm—a double reed, wind-capped predecessor to the oboe and bassoon, popular in the Medieval and Renaissance periods.

Silicon Pads—a durable pad with a silicon surface used on bassoons.

Sonic welding —high-frequency sound waves used to install posts on plastic instrument bodies.

Sound Production—the process unique to each instrument used to generate sound.

Spatula—the fingered part of a bassoon key.

Spring—strips of various metal alloys used to return a bassoon key to its rest position.

Step-Up (Intermediate)—the next step-up in quality and workmanship from a student-level musical instrument.

Student-Level—the least expensive entry-level musical instrument.

Tenon—the projection that joins each section of a bassoon.

Tone Holes—holes in the body of a bassoon used to change pitches.

Transposition—changing any combination of notes to a different key.

Triple Reed—a reed with three blades.

Tuning—the act of adjusting the pitch of an instrument.

Windcap—a cylinder that encapsulates a double reed.

Wing Joint—the first section of a bassoon's body after the bocal.

NOTES

An Index of Bassoon Parts with Reference Page Numbers

Bassoon Sections, 1

A. bocal

B. wing or tenor joint

C. boot or double joint

D. bass or long joint

E. bell joint

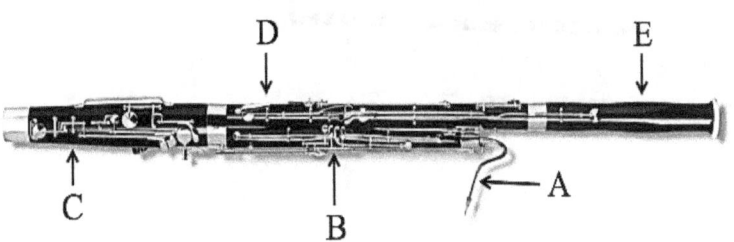

Bridge Keys, 95

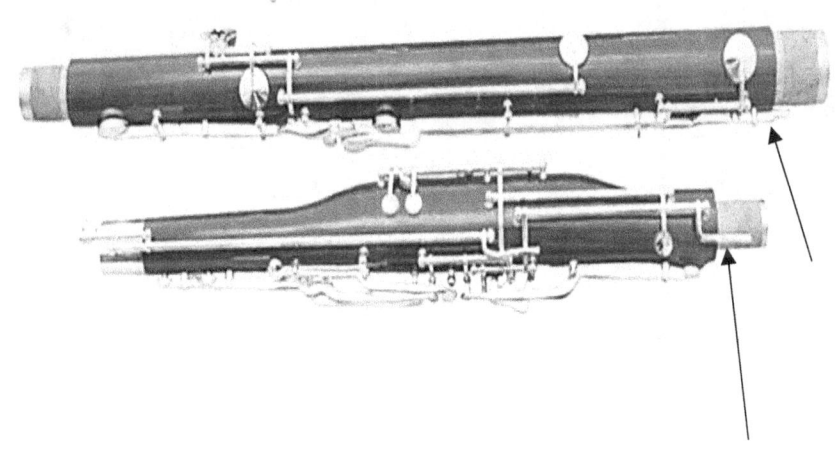

Leather Pad, 87, 92

Key Pad Cup, 86

Key Springs, wire, needle, flat, 87

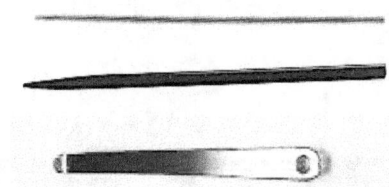

Paddle (spatula), 88, 93

Post, 27

Key System, 7

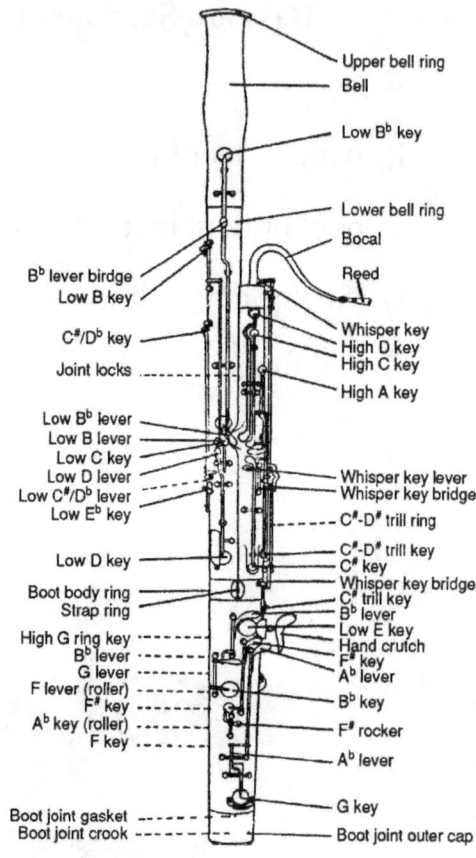

Reed, 3

Tenon, 1

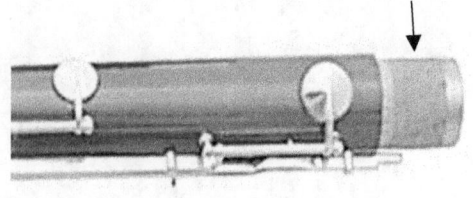

Tone Hole, 2

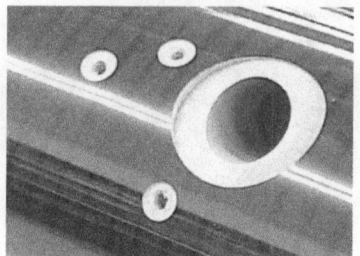

Instrument Ownership Record

This section is designed to document the history and maintenance of an instrument. By entering all the relevant information regularly, you will have a reference for periodic maintenance, information for a possible sale in the future, and a history of the instrument. Not every category listed will be relevant to every instrument. Fill in relevant information and add any information that suits your particular situation.

(Instrument) _____

Instrument's History

Owner's name _____

Date of purchase _____

Where purchased _____

Brand _____

Model and number _____

Date made _____

New [ ] previously owned [ ]

Previous owner(s) name(s) _____

Identifying marks, labels, serial number _____

Seller's Information

Name_____

Address_____

Phone_____

Email_____

Website_____

List or asking price_____

Price paid_____

Maintenance Record

When making an entry, include the date, action, repair, replacement or service, part serviced, brand or description of replacement part, source, technician's name, and contact information. Keep all invoices in a file for future reference.

General Service

DATE	SERVICE	TECHNICIAN	COST

Major Repairs

Detail the date, damage, cause, how repaired, by whom, and cost.

DATE	DESCRIBE REPAIR	COST	TECHNICIAN

Index

Appendix, 79
adjustment screws, 85
aulos, 48–49, 85
Baroque, 47, 59, 62, 85
bass joint, 85, 91
bassoon, (history) 61–63
bell, 1, 21, 52, 55, 60, 62, 65, 85, 91, 95
billet 21–22, 85, 91
bore, 2, 5, 17, 21–24, 28–29, 31–33, 38, 47, 58–63, 65, 85, 89, 91
care, 29–39
cases, 74–76
chalumeau, 50–52, 62
clarineo, 85, 91
clarinet, 14, 17, 51–55
Classical, 48, 59, 85
closed hole, 85, 87
conservatory system, 60, 85
cork pads, 85
crumhorn, 50, 86, 91
dictionary of bassoon termes, 91
dulcian, 61
ebonite, 24, 86, 91
facing, 86–87
fingering, 9–13
fipple, 46–47
fish skin, 86–87, 92
flute (history), 45–48, 54, 82, 85
glossary of woodwind instruments, 97
Grenadilla, 24, 86, 91
harmonics, 81–83, 86, 92
history, 45–64
Hotteterre, 46, 59, 62

key pad cup, 86–87, 92, 95
key system, 2, 6–7, 17–20, 24, 36, 46, 52, 54–55, 58–60, 63, 74, 85, 95–96
kinder Klari, 87
lay, 3–6, 87
leather pads, 52, 78, 92
ligature, 52–53, 87
lower Joint, 22, 87
made, (bassoons), 1, 3, 21–28
mouthpiece, 3, 14, 56–57, 85–89, 91
oboe, (history) 17–18, 47–48, 58–60, 85–86, 91-92
oil, 32–38, 65–66
ophicleide, 55
pad, 28, 37–38, 85–88, 92, 95
paddle, 86–87, 91–92, 96
pitch, 22–23, 46–50, 53, 67–68, 73, 79, 81–83, 86–89, 91–93
plateau keys, 60, 87
posts, 18, 23, 26–27, 34–36, 87–88, 92, 93, 96

reed, 1, 3–4, 14, 49, 51–52, 72–74, 85–87, 81–93, 96
rib, 88
saxophone (history) 55–57
science of sound, 79
shawm, 9–10, 200
side rails, 88
silicon, 88, 92
sonic welding, 27, 88, 93
sound production, 3, 73, 88, 93
spatula, 5, 88, 93, 96

Spring, 18, 27–28, 34, 37–38, 86–88, 91–93, 96
staple, 5, 89
step-up, 89, 93
student-level, 89, 93
tenon, 1, 27–29, 33–34, 89, 93, 96
throat, 57, 89
tip rail, 89
tone holes, 2, 5–6, 8–10, 17–18, 22–23, 28, 45–47, 49, 51–56, 61–62, 87, 89, 92–93
transposition, 15, 89, 93
tuning, 67–68, 89, 93
upper Joint, 89
windcap, 49–50, 58–59, 86, 89, 91, 93
window, 57, 89
wing joint, 1, 17, 30, 71, 89, 93
zummara, 50, 89